TODAY WE ENCOUNTER

A HARD SAYING

FR. IVOR KRAFT

TODAY WE ENCOUNTER
A HARD SAYING

The Lord, The Scripture, and Us

atelier≡ VIGILATE

ISBN-13: 978-1466258891

Today We Encounter a Hard Saying is a collection of
twenty-one sermons given by Fr. H. Ivor Kraft from 2007
to 2011 at St. Michael's by-the-Sea Episcopal Church in
Carlsbad, California USA

Sermons 1–20 transcribed by Craig Klampe

Cover Art
Front: Dome of the Church of the Holy Sepulchre, Jerusalem
Courtesy of http://en.wikipedia.org
Back: word cloud of this book
Courtesy of http://www.wordle.net

Source audio is available at stmichaelsbythesea.org

CONTENTS

PREFACE

In the late spring of 2011 Craig Klampe, a close friend and brother in Christ, handed me a volume of sermons. To my utter astonishment it was a collection of my own sermons preached during the past few years at St. Michael's by the Sea Episcopal Church in Carlsbad California. Craig served for many years as choirmaster at my former parish and has listened to me preach for twenty years. No record of my homiletic efforts exists, except some audio recordings made by St. Michael's. Realizing this, Craig, in a remarkable act of friendship, decided to rectify this by transcribing, from the recordings, the sermons found in this volume. This involved, among other things, looking up the passages of Holy Scripture quoted or alluded to but not cited in the sermons themselves. He has also sought to retain the patterns of oral delivery rather than edit them so as to turn them into essays. He hasn't told me how long all this took and I haven't asked. What I have tried to do is express my profound appreciation and gratitude which no words can actually convey. I hope you enjoy reading these sermons as much as I enjoyed delivering them.

Father Ivor Kraft
The Feast of Sts. Peter & Paul
June 29, 2011

PART I

Searching the Scriptures

1

A Hard Saying

In the name of the true and living God, the
Father, the Son, and the Holy Spirit.

Last Sunday, while teaching the adult forum, I made
an assertion that could easily have been misconstrued.
I said that Christianity, unlike Judaism and Islam, was
not a religion of a book, but of a person. Or to put it
another way, our Lord Jesus Christ, the eternal Son of
God, did not become man born of a virgin, live among
us as one of us, offer Himself on the cross to be raised
from the dead on the third day and ascend to His God
and our God, to His Father and to our Father in order
to give us... a book. He did all that so that He might give
us... Himself.

He made all of this as clear as I believe He possibly
could have, when He said to those who had determined
to put Him to death,

> You search the scriptures (by which He meant the Law
> and the Prophets), because you think that in them you
> have eternal life. And it is they that bear witness to me.
> Yet you refuse to come to me that you may have life.
> (Jn 5:39-40)

So let me repeat. The Lord came not to give us a book, but Himself. Nevertheless, this does not mean that we could do without the book. And that's where the misunderstanding can so easily arise. The Old and New Testaments—the sacred writings of the Old Israel and the New—are integral and indispensable to our religion and to each of us who adhere to it because they bear witness to our Lord. They are about Him. And He speaks to us through them, to us and to everyone everywhere, in all times and in all places, who will listen for His voice. This is the experience of the Jewish people through the centuries, and of Christians from the very beginning. In the words of our Lord, "Heaven and earth will pass away, but my words will not pass away." (Mt 24:35) And by this He does not mean only His words quoted directly in the four canonical gospels of Matthew, Mark, Luke, and John. For it is He Himself Who speaks to us through Moses, the Prophets, and the Apostles.

To say this is so, troubles people. And to say that it troubles people is to engage in understatement. Denying the clear and unequivocal meaning of our Lord's words—spoken directly, or indirectly through the Prophets and Apostles—has been a virtual industry from the beginning of the Church until now, and it will remain so. Sometimes naked self-interest is the obvious reason. The Lord's words stand in the way of my appetites, my inclinations, and I refuse to be limited by Him. I will accept no prohibition.

And so I pervert the word of the Lord. I twist it, deny that He actually said it or meant it, or I relegate it to the past. (That's very popular these days, right? "That was then. This is now!" And 'now' is a fictional time when the word of the Lord has passed away and whatever I want, or whatever I do, or whatever I believe, has mysteriously become permissible.)

It's also true that our Lord says disturbing things, things that are deeply troubling, and not only to those inside and outside the church who want to divinize themselves and legitimize their aberrant behavior. Consider our Lord telling His disciples that if they want to have His life in them they have to eat His flesh and drink His blood. The apostle St. John tells us that after He said this, the Lord's disciples said, "This is a hard saying. Who can listen to it?" (Jn 6:60) And after that many of them deserted Him.

I often imagine, you know, the preacher who gets up and tells the truth and loses a lot of his parishioners. Or the man who tells the truth and loses his friends. The truth is a difficult matter. By the way, through the last two thousand years, there have been Christians trying to explain away our Lord's words about eating His flesh and drinking His blood saying, 'He didn't really mean that.'

Today we encounter a hard saying. And I'm referring to the word of the Lord spoken by the apostle Paul in the reading from First Corinthians, a word that I couldn't avoid or evade when I was preparing for this morning.

> Everyone should remain in the state to which he was called. Were you a slave when called? Never mind.
> (1Cor 7:20-21)

Well, if I would have been there, I would have said to Paul, "That's easy for *you* to say."

It sounds like a callous thing to say, a sign of indifference to the slave. And because of these words and some others of St. Paul and also of St. Peter, there have been people who have wanted to claim that Christianity approves or, even worse, supports slavery. Some of them have been Christians wanting to justify their own behavior, and others have been enemies of Christ who want to discredit Christianity. And of course they are both wrong.

And then there are those who quote these words and say, "You see? The Bible... Well, there are a lot of things in the Bible we have to ignore today. There are words that are irrelevant; there are words that are just plain wrong. Or there are words that are time-bound." And all of this could not be further from the truth. Remember, the word of the Lord is for all people, at all times and in all places.

❦

Slavery is symptomatic of the fall of man. And it has been with us since the fall. And it will be with us until the Lord returns in glory, as will murder, theft, disease, death, and idolatry. If you read the scripture at all, you will know that Israel was enslaved in Egypt by the Pharaoh and put to hard labor. Slavery has existed on every continent among every people and every culture and in every civilization. And after a long and arduous struggle, a struggle which took not decades but centuries which included a terrible civil war in our own country, slavery was finally outlawed in the United States and throughout the Christian nations of the West, and also in places where Christian civilization held sway.

In a wonderful book, *Christianity On Trial,* by two men, Vincent Carroll and David Shiflett, we read that in British India, where as many as sixteen million were enslaved, it was made illegal to own a slave in 1862, the same year Abraham Lincoln announced the Emancipation Proclamation. While the 19th century was the century of abolition in the Christian West, this didn't mean the end of slavery. The story of the 20th century is the story of the rise of the omnivorous state, the state which wants to control everyone and everything, and usher in heaven on earth. It is the century of the utopian project. By the way, the 18th century Spanish philosopher Donoso Cortes said, "Imagined utopias produce real hells." And the 20th century certainly is the evidence of that truth.

And so it was that, when the Communist Party seized the Russian empire in 1917, the Party denounced private property as wicked, and revived slavery which had been done away with in the Christian Russian empire. It revived slavery, but as a state monopoly: private citizens can't be in that business but the state can own people.

The enslavement of the subjects of the Soviet empire began immediately after Lenin and his gang of criminals took over. And again from Carroll and Shiflett, the total number of slaves in forced labor camps during Stalin's regime alone (1927-1953) ranged up to 25 million, with the death rate at some camps estimated at 30% a year.

I commend to you the wonderful memoir of the terrible years of Soviet state slavery *Kolyma Tales* by Varlam Shalamov. This is a memoir of a man who survived 17 years as a slave in the northeast of Siberia in a forced labor camp in the Soviet Union where it is estimated that three million people perished in that one camp alone—one of the most notorious.

Today we can be certain that there have been and probably still are millions of slaves in China, North Korea, Cuba, and Vietnam, for slavery and Marxism go hand in hand, beginning to end.

And then there is the German national socialist slave system, also a state monopoly which followed the Marxist state slave system. The Nazis were notorious for having over the gates of the slave labor camps the slogan, "Work Makes Free." So that the slaves could meditate on that, no doubt, in their confinement and in their labors.

And slavery has always been integral to Islam, and has never been renounced among the Muslims. I suspect that we could find slaves in every Muslim country, chattel slaves, people owned by people. But two nations stand out, Mauritania and Sudan. I quote again from Carroll and Shiflett,

> In the 1990s Mauritania almost certainly held more slaves on a per capita basis than any other nation on earth, typically blacks owned by North African Arabs. (Again,) In early 2000 Solidarity International estimated that the number of Sudanese slaves topped 100,000. Most were Christian and animist black Africans from the Dinka tribe captured and transported to Arab and Muslim northern Sudan.

All of this is public knowledge, but it is not talked about. We don't hear about it. We don't discuss it. It is deeply disturbing, most troubling, and I don't recount all this to disturb you or to trouble you. But it's necessary to go through this to inform you, since there seem to be so few in our society that will inform us about these things. I need to inform you about these things so that we might understand the word of the Lord spoken through St. Paul.

Our Lord lived, died, and rose again to give Himself to everyone, slave as well as free. Whatever our state in life, whatever our condition, the Lord wants to dwell in us, and He wants us to dwell in Him.

> Everyone should remain in the state in which he was called. Were you a slave when you were called? Never mind. But if you can gain your freedom, avail yourself of the opportunity. For he who was called in the Lord as a slave is a freedman of the Lord. Likewise, he who was free when he was called is a slave of Christ. You were bought with a price. Do not become slaves of men. (1Cor 7:20-23)

To those enslaved by men—and despite our convictions as Christians, and our very best efforts, some men will always be enslaved by other men—this word is not a hard, indifferent, cold word. It is a word of the Lord, a word of life and hope.

Amen.

2

The Theological Meaning of History

In the name of the Father, and of the Son,
and of the Holy Spirit.

As some spoke of the Temple, how it was adorned with noble stones and offerings, he said, "As for these things which you see, the days will come when there shall not be left here one stone upon another that will not be thrown down."

Lk 21:5-6

Buildings, homes, places of worship, places of work and recreation are places of practical necessity, and all of them are at the same time symbols. And in the history of the world, there have been few buildings as potently symbolic as the Jerusalem Temple. The first Temple was built by Solomon, David's son and heir, in the tenth century BC. That Temple

19

was destroyed by the Babylonians.

In the year 586 BC, Jerusalem fell to Nebuchadnezzar and his armies, and he removed all the sacred objects from the Temple and burned it to the ground. And it was in that terrible event that the Ark of the Covenant was lost to history. The leaders of Israel were carried off into the famous Babylonian Captivity and after Babylon fell, they were allowed to return to Jerusalem and to the Promised Land. And in 537 BC, they began to rebuild the Temple.

It was not a very grand edifice and you can read about it in the books of Nehemiah and Ezra. But in 20 BC, twenty years before the birth of our Lord, Herod the Great began to dismantle that second Temple in order to build a truly grand edifice, a great Temple on the site of the first two. And this is the Temple that was still under construction during the lifetime of our Lord Jesus Christ.

The importance of the Temple can't be overstated. It was for Israel literally the house of God, the locus of God's presence in the world and in the midst of His people Israel. It was therefore the place of worship, the only place where the sacrifices given by God in the book of Leviticus could be offered, and therefore the only place where the priesthood of Israel could function and fulfill its ministry.

The synagogues were, as they are to this day, houses of study presided over by a teacher, or rabbi, who teaches Torah, especially the first five books of the Bible, the books of Moses. The Temple symbolized the religious heart of Israel not only for the Jews in the nation of Israel but for Jews throughout the world.

It might help us, two thousand years later, to grasp something of the significance of the Temple, by remembering September 11th, 2001. On that day, nineteen Muslim terrorists hijacked four commercial jetliners in a carefully planned and coordinated attack on our nation. They sought to destroy at least three structures that symbolized our country and its role in the world.

They succeeded in destroying the World Trade Center; they sought to destroy, but only damaged, the Pentagon; and thanks to the courage and determination of the passengers on the fourth plane, they failed to destroy as they had planned and hoped, either the Capitol building or the White House.

The goal clearly was not simply to destroy lives and property, but to traumatize and demoralize us as a people by destroying the most potent symbols of our economic, military, and political prowess. And you can imagine how terrible it would have been, and traumatizing it would have been, had they succeeded in that.

Now if you took the World Trade Center, the Pentagon, the White House, and the Capitol and rolled them all together, you would have something equivalent to the symbolic meaning of the Temple to the Jews in the time of our Lord and before. And so when the Lord speaks about the Temple, He is speaking about something of absolute significance and symbolic importance to His listeners.

> As some spoke of the Temple, how it was adorned
> with noble stones and offerings, He said, "As for these
> things which you see, the days will come when there
> will not be left here stone upon stone, that will not be
> thrown down."

These words form the introduction to what could be called Jesus' view of world history that will take place after Him. The promise of the destruction of the Temple forms a prelude, or an introduction, to the theological meaning of the events of history according to our Lord Jesus Christ. Regarding this history our Lord, after predicting the destruction of the Temple and all that that would mean, predicts three things: [the first being] false messiahs appearing with new gospels—"many will come in my name saying, 'I am he and the time is at hand.'" But we've seen that for the last two thousand years and we see it in our own time and it will continue to occur, and the Lord tells us bluntly, "Do not follow them." (Lk 21:8)

The second thing He tells us is that we will hear of wars and rumors of wars. "Kingdoms will rise against kingdoms, nations against nations, furthermore there will be great earthquakes, and in various places famines and pestilences, and there will be terrors and great signs from heaven." Well, we've witnessed these things throughout history, and we witness them right now, and we will continue to witness them. And the Lord tells us, "Do not be terrified." (Lk 21:9-11) In an age of the terrorist, that's a good word from the Lord.

Finally, He tells us to expect persecutions, and there have been persecutions of the faithful in every generation including our own, and they will not cease. The only thing that could possibly end the persecution of Christians would be our disappearance from the face of the earth.

"Gospel" means good news, and none of this sounds too good. Not exactly a lot of happy talk here from the Lord. False messiahs seeking to lead us astray with false gospels, war, famine, pestilence, and persecution—this is world history according to our Lord, and you may have noticed that He does not subscribe to a doctrine of progress. But before we see all this as simply negative, I ask you to consider that what the Lord predicted is what has actually happened and does happen and will happen. In other words, the Lord speaks to us with total frankness and honesty. And that is good news.

The Jerusalem Temple was destroyed in AD 70 just six years after it was finished and it took eighty-four years to complete the Temple. Our Lord cleansed that Temple, the Temple in Jerusalem, declaring it to be His Father's house and a house of prayer. But He also replaced the Temple with

His Own body when He declared, "Destroy this temple and in three days I will raise it up." (Jn 2:19) St. John tells us that He spoke of the temple of his own body. (Jn 2:21) Jesus Himself, he tells us, is the locus of the divine presence in the world (Jn 1:14), and therefore He is the temple not made by human hands. (Mk 14:58)

Our Lord Jesus Christ, the word of God made flesh, Whose body is the temple of God, has united us with Himself so that we can be His body, as the Apostles tell us, and therefore we are the temple of God made, in the words of St. Peter,

> of living stones built into a spiritual house to be a holy priesthood, to offer spiritual sacrifices acceptable to God through Jesus Christ. (1Pet 2:5)

And St. Paul tells us that we are God's temple because God's Spirit dwells in us. (1Cor 3:17)

> If anyone destroys God's temple, God will destroy him, for God's temple is holy and that temple you are.

So, what is the theological meaning of history according to our Lord?

The theological meaning of history according to our

24

Lord is this: that the creation is at war with its creator, the world is at war with the God Who made it, the Father, Son, and Holy Spirit. And we have been called out of the world to be in the midst of the world as the locus of the presence of God in the face of the world's enmity against God and the warfare that the creation has declared on the Creator. The Lord tells us simply that we must be tenacious and persistent and faithful to the end. Therefore He tells us to endure. And that's what we need in the midst of the world as His people, as His temple: we need endurance. For in the words of the apostle St. Paul in today's reading from the letter to the Galatians, "We must never weary in well-doing." (Gal 6:9)

Amen.

3

Seeing Isn't Believing

In the name of the Father, the Son,
and the Holy Spirit.

Thanks to Fr. Moquin, I was able to spend Holy Week and Easter on retreat at Nashotah House, the Anglo-Catholic seminary in Wisconsin. Both Fr. Moquin and Fr. Doran are graduates of the House, and have often told me what a wonderful place it is. I believed them, and so I was looking forward to going there, being on retreat and seeing for myself. I wasn't disappointed, although I did think it very strange not to be here with all of you in Holy Week and Easter.

Today is sometimes called 'Doubting Thomas' Sunday because every year on the Sunday after Easter Sunday we read St. John's account of the encounter between Thomas, the other apostles, and our Lord Jesus Christ. But before getting to that, I want to quote another Thomas, a Thomas who lived about a thousand years later, St. Thomas Aquinas, the philosopher and theologian who made this most relevant observation: It is better to see than to hear.

℮

It is better to see than to hear. And this is so because the one who sees, knows—while the one who hears, believes. Put another way, in order for there to be a believer—one who hears—there must be one who has seen—and knows. The one who sees speaks of what he knows, and the one who hears shares—or participates—in what has been seen, by believing what the one who has seen tells him.

Belief is not something other than knowledge. It is a participation, or sharing, in knowledge. It is a form of knowledge. While growing up I often heard people say 'seeing is believing,' but that's false. Seeing is knowing! *Hearing* is believing. For years, I've *heard* about Nashotah House, and I believed what I heard. I no longer believe it's a wonderful place. I've been there, seen it, and I now *know* that it's a wonderful place and can tell others who, if they believe me, will share in my knowledge of the place, as I once shared in Fr. Moquin's and Fr. Doran's knowledge by believing them.

On the first Sunday we call Easter, the Lord appeared to His disciples who had seen Him die a terrible death in public. And when He appeared to them three days later, He showed them His hands and His side. In other words, He exhibited the wounds. The wounds are the crucial and critical evidence that the One Who appeared to them is the very same One that they had seen die on Friday. The wounds are all.

Thomas is not among them when they see Him, and they tell him, "We have seen the Lord." Thomas very famously doubts, saying,

> Unless I see in His hands (and you'll notice he doesn't say 'unless I see HIM'—he wants to see the WOUNDS) the print of the nails and place my finger in the mark of the nails and place my hand in His side, I will not believe. (Jn 20:25)

And the question is, What is it that he will not believe unless he sees the Lord and touches the wounds?

Eight days later, the Lord again appears to the disciples. This time Thomas is present and the Lord says to him, "Put your fingers here and see My hands, and put out your hand and place it in my side." In the middle ages, it was a favorite subject of artists, you know: Thomas putting his hand into the wound in the Lord's side. And then the Lord says, "Do not be faithless, but believing." (Jn 20:27) Thomas is not asked to believe that the Lord has been raised from the dead. He now sees the Lord in the glory of the resurrection, and can *touch* Him with his own hands. Thomas does not doubt that Jesus is alive; he now *knows* that He is alive. When the Lord says, "Do not be faithless but believing," he cannot possibly mean 'believe that I've risen from the dead.'

Remember what the disciples said to Thomas after they saw Jesus and His wounds and received the Spirit from Him. They said to Thomas, "We have seen the Lord." Thomas, I think, may well have believed that they had seen Jesus risen from the dead. What he will not believe unless *he* sees Him, and sees the wounds that certify that it is the same Jesus they all saw die on Friday—what he will not believe until he sees Him and touches Him—is that Jesus is Lord.

When he sees Jesus, and when Jesus says to him, "Do not be faithless, but believing," Thomas responds saying, "My Lord and my God." (Jn 20:28) He does not say, "Well gosh, now I believe you have risen from the dead," because he knows he's risen from the dead! What he *believes*, on the basis of having seen the Lord in the resurrection is, now he believes *that Jesus is Lord and God.* The Lord responded to Thomas saying, "Do you believe because you have seen me? Blessed are those who have not seen and yet believe." (Jn 20:29) And now I want to repeat that, putting in the words that the Lord leaves out but which are implicit and crucial.

> The Lord said to Thomas, "Have you believed that I am Lord and God because you have seen me risen from the dead? Blessed are those who have not seen me risen from the dead and yet believe that I am Lord and God."

This blessing is for us, for you and for me. The Apostles and the first disciples of the Lord saw the Lord in the glory of the resurrection just as they had seen him die on the cross. St. Paul tells us that as many as five hundred saw the risen Lord. By believing them we share in their knowledge of the resurrection in exactly the same way that I shared in Fr. Moquin's and Fr. Doran's knowledge of Nashotah House by believing what they told me about that place.

To believe Jesus, the son of Mary, was raised from the dead is to share, or participate, in the knowledge of the first disciples of Jesus who saw and then told us what they had seen so that we can hear and believe them. But from that knowledge we are called to believe not simply what they saw and participate in their knowledge of the resurrection. We are called to believe that Jesus, the son of Mary, is the Son of God, our Lord Who has been exalted to the right hand of the Father and given the Name above every name.

It is better to see than to hear. In order for there to be a believer there must be a knower. In the case of Thomas's belief, and yours and mine, that Jesus is Lord and God, *who is the knower?* When we believe the apostles and disciples, we are believing them because they saw the Lord die and they saw Him in the glory of the resurrection. And so we can share. They have knowledge. They know, and when we believe them, we can participate in their knowledge. *But...*

> *who knows that Jesus is Lord and God in order that Thomas, and you and I, might believe and participate in that knowledge?*

And the answer is that the one who sees and knows is the One who raised Jesus from the dead. When our Lord said to Thomas, "Do not be faithless, but believing," He was asking Thomas to believe God, the God Jesus called 'Father,' the God Who called Jesus 'My beloved Son, with Whom I am well pleased.' (Mt 17:5) When we believe that Jesus is Lord and God, we are participating in the knowledge of God, Who *knows* the Son, and the Son Who knows the Father in the Spirit.

It is better to see than believe. We heard, in that very long reading that opens the book of Revelation, St. John tell us,

> Behold, He is coming with the clouds. And every eye
> will see Him. (Rev 1:7)

And that's our hope, that we will pass from believing to seeing, from believing to knowing. St. John writes in his first letter,

> Beloved, we who believe and are baptized are God's
> children now. It does not yet appear what we shall be,
> but we know that when He appears we shall be like
> Him for we shall SEE HIM AS HE IS. (1Jn 3:2)

That's the promise that has been made to us. We live in the

age of belief, the age of hearing. (That's one of the reasons sermons are big things in churches, hm?) We live in the time of hearing and believing. But the promise is that we will one day see and know because it is better to see than to believe. St. Paul therefore tells us that while we yet live in this interim, the age of hearing and believing, that one day, we will see. "Now," the apostle wrote to the Corinthians,

> we see through a glass dimly, but when He appears, we shall see Him face to face. And we shall know, even as we have been known. (1Cor 13:12)

In the meantime—in the meantime—we, who have not seen the Lord in the glory of the resurrection as the first disciples did, yet believe He is Lord and God, receive His blessing. And the blessing is: life in His name.

Amen.

4

The Good Samaritan

In the name of the Father, the Son,
and the Holy Spirit.

When I was in high school, I discovered a storyteller, a man named Jean Shepherd, and he told wonderful tales of his childhood and youth. He never became famous and I always regretted that because I thought he deserved fame. In fact, I bought a recording of his in which he tells a lot of stories and the title of the recording is, *Will Failure Spoil Jean Shepherd?* However, he has achieved a kind of immortality because he is the creator of *A Christmas Story,* not *the* Christmas story about the baby Jesus, the manger and the angels and the shepherds, but *A Christmas Story* about Ralphie, the little boy who wants the Red Ryder repeating carbine BB Gun for Christmas, and whose mother immediately says, "You'll put your eye out!" Which is exactly what my mother would have said, and all my friends' mothers.

So I resonated to that story; and what Shep (all his fans and all who love him call him "Shep") did is, he had all these stories of his childhood, which were woven together into that movie *A Christmas Story*, all built around the story of the BB gun, and he does the voice over in the film. Unfortunately for all the times that movie is shown every Christmas (and one cable network I think shows it 24 hours in a loop so you can hardly miss it) but very few people know that that's Shep doing the voice over and he's the creator of all the stories, and they're really all about him. At least, that's what he always told us.

My favorite story of Shepherd's, however, is not in that movie. It's about Shep when he's older; he's in high school. And a friend of his comes to him and says that he knows a girl that he wants to take to the movies but she won't go to the movies with him unless he can find a date for her girlfriend Helen, and would Shep please take Helen to the movies so that he can take the other girl to the movies. And Shep is indignant! He says, "What? A blind date?" he says. "I'm a kid of class!" he says. "I don't take girls out that can't get dates for themselves, that nobody wants to go out with." But his friend importunes him and finally, finally he agrees; he'll do it for his friend. Friday night he goes to the house to pick up the girl; her parents invite him in, he's waiting for her and she comes down the stairs and as she comes down the stairs he realizes she's beautiful, and he can't believe his eyes. And when he's introduced to her, he also quickly realizes that she is really nice, and he's ecstatic. And they go and meet their friends and they get a streetcar to the theater, and Shep says, "I sat on the aisle side of the seat to protect her from gum wrappers." And he said, "I was telling her all the family lore, you know? Like about how last winter the old man forgot to put antifreeze into the car and cracked the block!" And he said, "She's listening to my story very attentively… and suddenly I knew. Suddenly I understood. *I'm the blind date! They're all being nice to me.*"

Now believe it or not, this is relevant to today's Gospel. Trust me!

Our Lord is tested by a lawyer. Now, when we hear that "by a lawyer," we shouldn't think of Deacon Fred or my daughter and her husband, or Father Doran's brother or all the other lawyers we may know. By a "lawyer" it means a rabbi, what we would call a rabbi, a teacher of the Law, and the Law is the first five books of the Old Testament or the Jewish scripture, the books of Moses: Genesis, Exodus, Leviticus, Numbers, and Deuteronomy. A lawyer is someone who knows the Law and teaches it.

And so this rabbi tests the Lord and asks Him the great question, "What must I do to inherit eternal life?" (Lk 10:25) And this is exactly, by the way, the question asked by that individual generally known as the Rich Young Ruler who comes to the Lord and says, "What must I do to inherit eternal life?" (Lk 18:18) And since the man is a teacher of the Law, a rabbi, the Lord asks him what he reads in the Law. And the man quotes Deuteronomy 6:4, "You shall love the Lord your God with all your heart, mind, soul, and strength." And then he quotes Leviticus 19:18, "You shall love your neighbor as yourself." And the Lord says, "You have answered right. Do this and you'll live." (Lk 10:25-28) In other words, 'Since you know the answer, why did you ask?' That's really what the Lord is saying to him.

And now, Luke tells us that the man needed to justify himself for asking the question he knew the answer to, since he didn't want information, he didn't want to learn anything, he wanted to put the Lord to the test, and so now he asks, "Well, who is my neighbor?" (Lk 10:29) And this question is also disingenuous because the neighbor that the Israelite is to love as himself is a fellow Israelite and that's clear from the book of Leviticus, the nineteenth chapter. And in response to this question, "Who is my neighbor?" the Lord tells the Parable of the Good Samaritan. (Lk 10:30-37)

It is natural for us to look for ourselves in the parables. You know, the Parable of the Prodigal Son is really all about the Father not the Son. (Not the Prodigal Son even, there's another son, okay?) But since we all want to find ourselves in the parables, we have made that parable into the Parable of the Prodigal Son rather than the Parable of the Loving Father. And so it is that in the Parable of the Good Samaritan, I immediately am looking for myself. Am I like that priest?

Oh, I hope not; I hope I'm not like him. He passes by on the other side and leaves the man half dead on the side of the road. But I suspect that I might be like him. It's a disconcerting thought.

And then there's the Levite; he does the same thing, he passes by on the other side. And the tribe of Levi is the tribe of Moses and his brother Aaron. Priests were descended from Aaron, the brother of Moses, Aaron being the first Israelite priest, and all of the members of the tribe of Levi had special religious responsibilities and duties just like all Christians.

Oh Lord, I don't want to be like the Levite, either.

And then we come to the Samaritan himself; the Samaritan is good beyond good. He's extravagantly good.

Now, I've helped some people in my day, at least I like to believe that I have, but I've never helped anybody like that, like the Samaritan helps the man by the side of the road. And as long as I'm looking for myself in the parable, I'm lost, because I really don't want to identify with the priest or the Levite, and I really can't identify with the Samaritan, even though I would like to.

And so the parable merely accuses me. As long as I'm looking for myself in the parable, I'm lost. The one I need to look for in the parable is our Lord. And when I look for the Lord, I then coincidentally find myself. The Good Samaritan is our Lord Jesus Christ; it is He Who is the neighbor to everyone and anyone who needs mercy. The parable is all about Him, and even though I'd like to believe it's all about me, the fact of the matter is it's really not. It is all about Him. And now a little like Shep on his blind date, I can recognize myself once I recognize Him. I'm the man who's dying, the man to whom our Lord proved to be a neighbor. Our Lord has mercy on all who need Him, offering life to all who are perishing and I'm one of those people and so are you.

And now we can go back to the rabbi's question, "What must I do to inherit eternal life?" because that's what occasions all of this. The Lord's answer to that question is the parable and its conclusion, "Go, and do likewise." This is not an exhortation to some kind of supernatural extravagant generosity; it is an invitation to share in the goodness, the love, and the mercy of the Lord Himself. It is an invitation to discipleship. It is our Lord Who loves God with His whole heart, mind, soul, and strength; and it is our Lord Jesus Christ Himself Who loves His neighbor as Himself, and His neighbor, He tells us in the parable, is anyone and everyone who needs Him, who needs His mercy, His generosity, and His goodness. And this is the key to the extravagant love we see in the parable, and to His own extravagant love and goodness and mercy, the love which loves "even unto death, death on a cross," to quote St. Paul in his letter to the Phillippians. (Phil 2:8)

The Lord's answer to the rabbi is an invitation to discipleship, for our Lord is Himself eternal life and He wishes to share His eternal life with everyone. And so the Lord's answer to the question, "What must I do to inherit eternal life?" is "Follow me."

Amen.

5

The Vineyard of the Lord

In the name of the Father, and of the Son,
and of the Holy Spirit.

Last Sunday at the conclusion of the Adult Forum, I was asked, perhaps providentially, to address a question at a future forum and the question was this: Why did God choose the Israelites? Now this actually is a terribly important question, for if we don't understand why He chose Israel, we won't understand why He has chosen us, for the Church is the new Israel, formed by the Lord God in Jesus Christ the perfect Israelite.

Well, to begin with, we need to understand that the Lord did not look around at all the peoples and nations He had made and said, "Well, I like them best. The Israelites, I'll choose them!" According to the biblical narrative, we read that the Lord chose Abraham, who was most certainly not an Israelite. He chose him for reasons known to Him alone, and from Abraham and his wife Sarah, He created a people. In the biblical view, a race or nation is a people with a common ancestor. Hence, all human beings are members of the human race, because we are all descended from a common ancestor, the first Adam. (Although it's rarely acknowledged, this view—which is foundational for western civilization—is not universally accepted.)

In any case, the Lord called Abraham and made a covenant of promise with him; he promised Abraham that he would have numberless descendants, that the Lord would give those descendants a land to dwell in, and that by Abraham and his descendants all the nations and peoples of the earth would be blessed. This covenant of promise was then made with Isaac (Abraham's son), and again with Abraham's grandson Jacob, and the Lord God changed Jacob's name to Israel. The Israelites are the descendants of a common ancestor Jacob, whose name was changed to Israel. One of Israel's twelve sons, by the way, was Judah, whose descendants are the Judaites, or more simply, the Jews.

We ourselves, having been born again of water and the Spirit, are adopted children of God through union with His only-begotten Son Jesus Christ. We have Him as, in a sense, our common ancestor and, therefore, are known as Christians, those who are in Christ, who are related to Him as His brothers and sisters.

In the reading from the prophet Isaiah, the Lord calls Israel His chosen and declares why He has created them to be His own particular possession among all the peoples of the earth.

> I give water in the wilderness, rivers in the desert, to give drink to my chosen people, the people whom I formed for Myself, THAT THEY MIGHT DECLARE MY PRAISE. (Is 43:20-21)

Now that's the punchline, that's what you have to hear. Why did he create this people from the seed of Abraham? So that they would declare His praise, and in declaring His praise, make Him known to the ends of the earth, to all the nations and peoples of the world.

I realize that all of this sounds like a lecture on biblical history better suited to the classroom than to the Mass but unless we have some clarity about all this, we'll have a difficult time understanding the Parable of the Vineyard (Lk 20:9-18) and the word the Lord wants to speak to us here and now.

The image of Israel as the Lord's vineyard is ancient and it's found in the prophets; and the people who heard the Lord speak the Parable of the Vineyard would have understood His meaning immediately.

The servants cast out and killed are the prophets who had been sent to Israel, the Lord's vineyard, through the years. And Jesus is the heir sent by the owner looking for fruit he planted the vineyard to produce. The accusation made by the Lord is that the tenants want the vineyard for themselves and so cast out the representatives of the owner whenever they appear and so will cast Him out in a brazen attempt to gain possession of the vineyard once and for all.

> The scribes and the chief priests tried to lay hands on Him at that very hour but they feared the people for they perceived that He had told this parable against them. (Lk 20:19)

The Lord's accusation is that they wanted to be the chosen but did not want the One Who chose them, they wanted the land of promise but not the One Who had promised it; in short, they wanted the gifts but they did not want the Giver.

Well, it's very easy to think about those terrible scribes and chief priests and their evil machinations, and then fall prey to the sin of the Pharisee who prays, when he sees the Publican, "Oh thank you Lord, that you didn't make me like that man!" The Church however, is the new Israel formed by a new covenant through faith in a sacramental sharing of the Lord's sacrificial death and resurrection, and our Lord Who spoke the Parable of the Vineyard two thousand years ago against the scribes and the chief priest has applied the image of the vineyard to Himself and to us. Hear the word of the Lord, as found in the fifteenth chapter of the Gospel of St. John.

> I am the true vine, and my Father is the vinedresser. Every branch of Mine that bears no fruit, He will take away; and every branch that does bear fruit, He prunes that it may bear more fruit. Abide in Me, and I in you; as the branch cannot bear fruit by itself unless it abides in the vine, neither can you, unless you abide in Me. I am the vine, you are the branches; he who abides in Me and I in him, he it is that bears much fruit, for apart from Me, you can do nothing. By this My Father is glorified that you bear much fruit and so prove to be My disciples. As the Father has loved Me so I have loved you; abide in My love. These words I have spoken to you that My joy may be in you, and that your joy may be full. (Jn 15:1-2,4-5,8-9,11)

We are the vineyard of the Lord. Like the old Israel, we've been formed by the Lord to declare His praise. Those are the words of the Lord spoken to ancient Israel through Isaiah, but listen to the word of the Lord spoken to us, the new Israel, through the apostle Paul.

> In Him according to the purpose of Him Who accomplishes all things according to the counsel of His will,

we who first hoped in Christ have been destined and ap-
pointed to live for the praise of His glory. (Eph 1:11-12)

And so it is that we must hear the Parable of the Vineyard
in light of our own vocation and with great humility. You
and I are called to abide in Christ. In the canon of the Mass,
we ask the Father to grant that by the reception of His Son's
most precious body and blood, we may be made one body
with Him that He may dwell in us and we in Him. And
hearing those words over and over again they become like a
white noise and it's easy to just let them go by. We who are
united with Christ, the apostle St. Peter tells us in his first
letter,

are a chosen race, a royal priesthood, a holy nation,
God's own people—(To what end?)—that we may
declare the wonderful deeds of Him Who called us out
of darkness into His own marvelous light. (1Pet 2:9)

We have been called out of darkness to declare the wonderful deeds of God, to live to the praise of His glory. And
we do this by abiding in the Son so that the Son can bear
fruit in us. We are a supernatural race and nation, but not
through genetics or biological descent.

You see, you can be born an Israelite; any one who
is a descendant of Israel is an Israelite, a Jew. But you can
never be born a Christian; we must be reborn by water and

the Spirit, share in the passion and death of our Lord, and therefore share also in His resurrection, so that He can dwell in us and we can dwell in Him, so that He can abide in us and we can abide in Him, to the end that all the nations and races of the world may come to know the Lord and share in His light and life, the light and life that we have been called to share in.

The truth is that you and I and everyone from the first Adam to the last is made from the dust of the earth to share in the life of the One Who made us all; we've been created to praise the glory of the Father in union with the Son, in the power and unity of the Holy Spirit.

Amen.

PART II

Got Bread?

6

The Work of God

In the name of the Father, and of the Son,
and of the Holy Spirit.

Once upon a time, I was a musician, a classical musician, an orchestral clarinetist but, like many of my friends, I was enamored of the language of the hipster and the jazz musician. And so it is that more times than I could possibly remember, I asked or was asked by friends, "Do you have any bread?" The answer was usually an emphatic "no!" Bread was the universal synonym for money, and forty years ago I never really considered how biblical that is, for bread, in holy scripture, is the symbol for all of what we need to sustain ourselves in this world, just as money is a symbol of all that we need to sustain ourselves in this world.

In the very brief prayer that our Lord Jesus Christ gives to us, that He teaches us to pray, He teaches us to ask our heavenly Father to sustain us, to provide all that we need in this life and in this world, by asking Him to give us our daily bread. Right? "Give us this day our daily bread," which includes everything: food, clothing, shelter, and that long and ever-growing list of things that we believe we need in order to survive in this world. We human beings are fragile, hungry creatures and we all know that without bread, actual or metaphorical, we will perish.

Today's Gospel follows the miraculous feeding of the five thousand in the wilderness after which our Lord, "perceiving that the people were about to come and take Him by force to make Him King, withdrew again to the hills by Himself." (Jn 6:15) You will recall that after His baptism, our Lord retreated into the wilderness for forty days and fasted, and during that time the devil drew near to Him and asked Him,

> If you are the Son of God, why die on the cross? Why not turn stones into bread and feed a perpetually hungry world?

To which our Lord responded by quoting the book of Deuteronomy, "Man does not live by bread alone, but by every word that proceeds from the mouth of God." (Mt 4:3-4, Deut 8:3) The devil however, as usual, knew what he was talking about. When our Lord fed the multitude with earthly bread, they flocked to Him; the same people who would later cry out for His death (right?), "Crucify Him!"—these people flock to Him, when He feeds them with earthly bread, to make Him King. But our Lord had already rejected that temptation in the wilderness. The bread He was sent to provide for us is Himself, and He would allow no other coronation than His crucifixion, when it would be announced to the whole world that He was King of the Jews in Hebrew, Greek, and Latin, when He was crowned with thorns. So when the crowd followed Him into that place to which He had withdrawn, He declared to them,

> Truly, truly I say to you, you seek Me not because you saw signs (that is, signs confirming My identity as the Messiah and Son of God), but because you ate your fill of the bread.

And then He added,

> Do not labor for the food which perishes but for the food which endures to eternal life which the Son of Man will give to you, for on Him God the Father has set His seal. (Jn 6:26-27)

Man does not live by bread alone, but by every word that proceeds from the mouth of God, and Jesus is the definitive word of God; He is, as St. John tells us, "He is the word of God made flesh." (Jn 1:14)

It would be easy to misunderstand our Lord. He is not telling us that we can live without earthly bread. In the Sermon on the Mount, He exhorts us to not be anxious about what we shall eat or what we shall drink or what we shall wear—not because these things are unimportant, but because our heavenly Father knows that we need them all and will provide them for us—but first, He says, to seek His righteousness and His Kingdom.

Our Lord does not underestimate or minimize our material needs. How could he? He created us, and not only that, He became one of us, He became a fully human being. And if He became a fully human being, that means He had to eat, because human beings have to eat earthly bread. And we know that He earned that bread by the sweat of His brow as a carpenter, and when He was thirty and began His public ministry, He was supported by offerings, and the Apostles had a treasurer, something that's easy to forget. I usually don't like to bring it up because Judas was the treasurer, and it can make the parish treasurer feel bad. But that's the fact: the Apostles had a treasurer, they needed money, they had to eat.

In Christian tradition, there are many stories that remind us that we must eat, literally and not simply spiritually. One of my favorite stories confirming this is found in the *Sayings of the Desert Fathers*. The desert fathers were the first monks;

they were men who went out into the deserts of Egypt and Syria when those countries were fervently Christian. They went out in the third century and after; they didn't go into monasteries because there was no such thing, there was no such thing as monasticism. These were mostly laymen and they went out into the desert to lead devout lives, to live simply, chastely, charitably, and above all, prayerfully. And one of my favorite figures from the desert is Abba John the Dwarf. Now with a name like that, he's got to be interesting. And he was, and his sayings, the sayings attributed to him, are wonderful; he was one of the most colorful figures in the desert. And he drew many people to himself, and was eventually ordained a priest. And this is one of the stories told about his early life, perhaps a story before he left his ancestral home to go into the desert.

> It was said of Abba John the Dwarf that one day, he said to his elder brother, "I should like to be free of all care, like the angels who do not work but ceaselessly offer worship to God!" So he took off his cloak and went away into the desert. After a week, he came back to his brother. When he knocked on the door, he heard his brother say before he opened it, "Who are you?" He said, "I am John, your brother." But he replied, "John has become an angel, and is henceforth no longer among men." Then John begged him saying, "It is I!" However, his brother did not let him in, but left him

53

> there in distress until morning. Then, opening the door,
> he said to him, "You are a man, and you must once
> again work in order to eat." Then John made a prostra-
> tion before him saying, "Forgive me."

Our Lord Jesus Christ did not become an angel, He became man, one of us. None of us are angels, that is, disembodied spirits who do not need to eat, but we are embodied souls who must eat to live. Therefore when our
Lord told the hungry multitude not to labor for the food
which perishes but for the food that endures to eternal
life, they immediately change the subject, and ask Him,
"What must we do to be doing the works of God?" (Clearly, when somebody is being as unreasonable and as un-
realistic as our Lord, the best thing to do is to move on!)
But our Lord was not about to let them change the subject
and so He answered, "This is the work of God (and note
that He went from the plural 'what must we be doing to
do the works of God?' to the singular 'this is the work of
God,' the definitive work of God) that you believe in Him
Whom He has sent."

"This is the work of God, that you believe in Him Whom
He has sent." In both the Greek and Latin languages, the
verb 'to trust' and the verb 'to believe' are the same word,
and therefore this could have been translated just as ac-

curately, and perhaps more helpfully, "This is the work of God, that you *trust* in Him Whom He has sent." This is the work of God that Israel refused to do in the wilderness when, upon finding themselves in a barren desert, they began to remember mythical food that they had when they were slaves, 'Oh, if only we were back in Egypt when we sat by the fleshpots and had bread to the full!' They had already forgotten what it was really like! (It's a little bit like when those of us who have reached our seniority start to remember the 'good old days,' right? 'Ah, remember how good it was!' No, it wasn't that good, *really*.) So they're out there and they're remembering all this food that they don't have, and what do they say? They do not trust Moses, whom the Lord had sent to them, but they say, "He has brought us out into this wilderness to kill us with hunger."

When our Lord warned His hearers that they could not serve God and mammon, the Pharisees ridiculed Him because, according to St. Luke, they were lovers of money. (Lk 16:13-14) Yet the question remains, "Is there anything more important than money, or earthly bread?"

Bernie Madoff and all the Bernie Madoffs of this world past, present, and future, don't think so. Why did he, and why do all those like him, steal when they have more than enough by any worldly standard? I often meditate on that. Bernie, if he woulda just stolen ten billion, he could have still got the big flat screen tv, two cars, taken a vacation every year, right? But no! He had to steal fifty billion! Which brings us to the question, "How much is enough?"

When the world's richest man, John D. Rockefeller, the Bill Gates of his day, was asked this question, it is said, and I like to believe that it's true (it's spiritually true), he was asked, "How much money is enough?" And Rockefeller supposedly responded, "More, just a little more." I remember the New Yorker had a cartoon like that, showing the executive kneeling before his wing chair at the fireplace praying, "More, just a little more."

When Kermit had the audacity to remind Miss Piggy (I hope all of you remember Miss Piggy) of the famous architect Mies van der Rohe's dictum, 'Less is more,' an outraged Miss Piggy said, "Less is not more, more is more!" You have to love Miss Piggy; she is the voice of the world.

All of which means that there is a hunger in us that is never satisfied no matter how much earthly bread we consume; and the sad and tragic sign of this is that the rich and famous, who appear to have all that would satisfy, kill themselves with shocking regularity, just like the poor and obscure. Our Lord calls us to labor above all for the food which He will give us, food that endures to eternal life, bread which comes down from heaven and gives life to the world; but in order to believe that such bread exists, we—the new Israel wandering through the wilderness of this world and always tempted to believe that the Lord has made us and then left us wandering in this wilderness simply to die—must do the work of God. And the work of God is to believe and to trust our Lord Jesus Christ.

Amen.

7

Everyone Needs Money

In the name of the Father, and of the Son,
and of the Holy Spirit.

I need money. Don't be alarmed. I'm not going to ask anyone to pass the plate on my behalf. I need money, and so do you. So does everyone everywhere. We need money because we need all those things that it can obtain, beginning of course with the absolute necessities of life: food, clothing, shelter. And from these basic necessities there comes an elaboration of things that we need. In order to eat, we not only need food, we need stoves, refrigerators, sinks, dishes, tables, tablecloths, napkins, silverware, salt and pepper. When my wife and I got married, I realized that in my parents' drawers there was a lifetime accumulation of those things that I didn't have. And my wife and I spent years and years collecting them all. Right? Can openers! Potato peelers!

You take all those things for granted until you have to provide for them yourself. We all need clothes, and therefore we need closets, hangers, drawers, irons and ironing boards, washers and dryers, not to mention places to keep them all. And that's just the beginning.

And so it is, that everyone everywhere needs money. The holy family needed money, and they obtained it through the labor of Joseph, the foster-father and guardian of our Lord Jesus Christ. Joseph was a village carpenter, often referred to simply as St. Joseph the Worker. And he taught his foster son, our Lord Jesus Christ, his trade.

Which brings me to something rarely ever mentioned. In fact, I never ever hear it mentioned. Our Lord Jesus Christ needed money. Have you ever pondered that? That's all part of His true humanity.

You know, being the Son of God in the flesh, He just didn't sit there and have money rain down on Him, or say, "Hey, I'm the Son of God! Take care of me!" He needed money, and He obtained it by working. He worked to support Himself and His widowed mother, the Blessed Virgin Mary. And those years of obscurity and labor are called His hidden life.

When He was about thirty years old, St. Luke tells us, He began His public ministry, which lasted about three years. And during that public ministry He did not work as a village carpenter as you know, He was traveling about the Holy Land (what we now call the Holy Land), and He was supported by His admirers and His disciples who provided for Him and the apostles, among them people like Joseph of Arimathea who was described both as a disciple and a rich man, a rich man who provided the tomb for our Lord. St. John tells us explicitly and more than once, that the Apostles and our Lord during their travels needed money, and they received it from people who supported them in their ministry. And Judas kept the money box. (I always like to make jokes about that vis-a-vis parish treasurers.)

In any event, holy scripture and our Lord Who speaks through it, is not a book of fairy tales detached from reality, and it is precisely because the Bible is a book of reality and our Lord is a teacher of truth, that our Lord and the whole biblical witness acknowledge the necessity of money, something we rarely talk about in church, especially not our Lord's need for it, but the reality is what it is.

However, holy scripture is also concerned to warn us about the dangers of money, because money does possess for us a danger. You know, my joke always is that if you won the lottery, it would be a grave spiritual danger for you; but if I won, I'd know how to handle it. Right? And we all believe that we'd know how to handle it. It's only dangerous for other people. And all those warnings in the scripture about money, its dangers and all the things that it buys don't really apply to us because, well, we're exempt from that.

Popular culture occasionally reminds us that wealth can be dangerous. I don't know how many of you remember *The Millionaire*. (I won't ask you to raise your hand.) Every week, the Millionaire (I think his name was John Beresford Tipton, Jr.) would pick out some person and give them a million dollars anonymously. And then we would all watch to see how it affected the person's life, all that wealth coming unexpectedly. It actually had a good moral, that program, a little different from *Lifestyles of the Rich and Famous*, which came a decade or two later. Right?

Money is necessary and it's also dangerous (a little like fire, I might add). We read in St. Luke that the Pharisees who were mortal enemies of our Lord, and who conspired to have Him murdered, were lovers of money. Judas, responsible for the money used by the apostles and our Lord, betrayed the Lord for money, reminding us that there are people always who will do anything, absolutely anything, for money.

Simon the magician sought to obtain the gift of God, namely the Holy Spirit, with money, reminding us that there are some things—there really are actually some things— money won't buy. (Acts 8:18-19)

The apostle Paul, who labored for the food he ate by making tents and who declared that those who would not work should not eat (2Thess 3:10), also stated emphatically

61

that the love of money is the root of all evil and he exhorts us to keep ourselves free from it. (1 Tim 6:9-11)

Please note the problem here is not money, but displaced love. And I go through all this because I believe it's necessary in order to understand the word of God for us today. "One of the multitudes said to Jesus, 'Teacher, bid my brother divide the inheritance with me.'" (Lk 12:13) Our Lord must have had great prestige for someone to ask Him to do this, since He was Himself a layman. He responded by pointing out that He had no authority to do any such thing, but added,

> Take heed and beware of all covetousness for a man's life does not consist in the abundance of his possessions. (Lk 12:15)

Here we have a cautionary word, encountered so often on the lips of our Lord and in the scriptural tradition. It's a cautionary word because money is so important that we all need it and therefore we are likely to inflate its significance and to define people by their possession or lack of it. "Take heed and beware of all covetousness for a man's life does not consist in the abundance of his possessions." Here we have a truly counter-cultural word, not only counter-cultural in our society but in every society that's ever existed. And after our Lord makes this pronouncement, He tells the parable known as the Parable of the Rich Fool. And the question we should all ask ourselves is, why is he a fool and why is he condemned?

𝒞

Well, if you listen carefully, you'll notice that he was not condemned because he was rich. That's almost coincidental. In fact, his situation is desirable. Through his labor, he has achieved a measure of economic security, and he can rest. Now, I don't know about you, but that's the retirement dream! It's certainly mine. It's what we would all hope for, right? To be economically independent so that we could rest from our labors. And again, the question is, what's the problem?

The answer is found in the word *covetousness*. "Beware of all covetousness, for a man's life does not consist in the abundance of his possessions." "Thou shalt not covet," is the tenth commandment. In the Roman Catholic and Lutheran enumeration of the commandments, it's both the ninth and tenth commandment. And the commandment is given to Israel—the old Israel—and to us, the new Israel, and through us to everyone, because covetousness destroys gratitude. It destroys gratitude and undermines our relationship with our creator and also our relationship with our neighbor.

When I covet, I do not thank God for all His blessings to me. Rather, I resent the fact that you have something I do not. Covetousness always produces envy, resentment, and ingratitude. It poisons us, it poisons our relationship with God, and it poisons our relationship with our neighbor, and in the second reading, from Colossians, the apostle Paul at the very beginning of that reading, if you look at it, equates covetousness with idolatry. (Col 3:5)

Well, we still have a problem. The man in the parable doesn't covet, does he? So what's the connection? The connection is this: the man in the parable is ungrateful. He does not speak to his Lord and God to praise Him for providing for him materially. Rather, he talks only to himself. He does not praise God for His goodness and generosity but plans his future as though God did not exist. Hence, he is in biblical terms, a fool. For the Psalmist teaches us that, "the fool says in his heart, 'there is no God.'" (Ps 14:1, 53:1) The man in the parable is turned in upon himself and in his interior dialogue, the personal pronoun occurs over and over. He is in actual practice an atheist, whether he goes to the synagogue or not.

Listen again to the parable. (Lk 12:16-19)

> The land of a rich man brought forth plentifully and he thought to himself, "What shall I do? For I have nowhere to store my crops." And he said, "I will do this. I will pull down my barns and build larger ones and there I will store up all my grain and my goods and I will say to my soul, 'Soul, you have ample goods laid up for many years. Take your rest. Eat, drink, and be merry.'"

This man lives as if there is no God, and so he is a fool, a rich fool, but a fool nonetheless. And the problem is not his wealth but his atheism which has destroyed his gratitude. To lay up treasure for oneself without being rich toward God means to be turned in upon the self, and therefore without gratitude toward the One from Whom all good things come, the One from Whom all blessings flow.

John Zizioulas, a Greek Orthodox bishop and a very great theologian, observes quite simply that atheism is a form of ingratitude. The Greek word *eucharistein* means to thank. We are here to offer the Holy Eucharist, the Holy Thanksgiving. Our Lord Jesus Christ is Himself the Eucharistic Man, the Man who attributes everything to God, the Son Who attributes everything to His heavenly Father. And we who believe and are baptized are His brothers and sisters. So let us beware of all covetousness, for a man's life does not consist in the abundance of his possessions. A man's life consists in the ability to recognize the One from Whom all good things come, and to say thank you.

Amen.

8

The Sacred Diet

In the name of the Father, the Son,
and the Holy Spirit.

It's the Lord's day, and the Lord is again talking to all of us about food, but then He very often is.

> The Lord your God is bringing you into a good land,
> a land of wheat and barley, of vines and fig trees and
> pomegranates, a land of olive trees and honey, a land in
> which you will eat bread without scarcity, a land where
> you shall eat and be full. (Deut 8:7-10)

So said the Lord to His people Israel through the prophet Moses. "Taste and see that the Lord is good; happy are they who trust in Him." So says the psalmist. (Ps 34:8) And our Lord declares of Himself, "I am the bread of life; I am the living bread which came down from heaven.

If anyone eats of this bread, he will live forever." (Jn 6:48,51)

If holy scripture is the reliable and authoritative means by which our Lord speaks to us, and it is, then He is clearly very concerned with what we eat. The Bible is about God, man, and food. Now, I know that doesn't sound right, but believe me, it's true.

When God made man, he immediately gave him a diet. "Every plant yielding seed which is upon the face of all the earth, and every tree with seed in its fruit, you shall have them for food." (Gen 1:29) He also added a famous dietary prohibition: "You may eat freely of every tree of the garden, but of the tree of the knowledge of good and evil you shall not eat, for in the day you eat of it you shall die." (Gen 2:16) The original sin is the desire to be God rather than to be His creature, but the really interesting thing is that the form that the original sin takes is eating. Man eats that which God has prohibited.

Having turned away from God into himself, man quickly turns to murder on a massive scale and the Lord cleanses the world by a flood and begins again with Noah and his family. And guess what? *He immediately prescribes a diet.* "Every moving thing that lives shall be food for you; and as I gave you the green plants, I give you everything." (Gen 9:3) And again, the Lord added a dietary prohibition: "Only you shall not eat flesh with its life, that is, its blood." (Gen 9:4)

Jacob and his family ended up in Egypt because of

a famine; they were starving and there was food in Egypt. More than four centuries later, when the Lord led Jacob's descendants, the Israelites, out of Egypt, He commanded the Israelites to prepare a sacred meal, the Passover meal, and to repeat it throughout all generations to commemorate the Exodus. Israel, once having left Egypt and entered into the wilderness, rebelled against the Lord. They murmured. (I've always liked that, they *murmured*.) And what did they murmur about? Well, they murmured about the food! The form of the rebellion against the Lord in the wilderness was about the food.

Well, the Lord fed them with manna, and as they journey to the land flowing with milk and honey, the land that had all that good food that we heard about in the first reading, He provided them with a detailed diet, which included many prohibitions. To this day, an observant Jew keeps kosher, the diet given to Israel in the wilderness, and among many other things abstains from eating pork.

All living things must eat in order to exist but, for human beings, food is about much more than survival. All living things eat to exist but we eat to live. We humans cook our food, we prepare it, we create intricate recipes, and food is essential to all festivity. Imagine Thanksgiving or Christmas or a birthday without the dinners. Imagine any real celebration without food. Sharing food creates a bond between people, and real friendship is unthinkable apart from shared meals.

And food is about identity: religious identity, cultural identity. Civilizations and cultures create cuisines; religions create the civilization and the culture, and the cultures produce food, cuisines. In America we have them all. I remember twenty years ago going to Europe for the first time and realizing I was in Italy and there was nothing to eat but Italian food. (Sounds ridiculous, doesn't it, when you think about it.) Then we went to Germany; my wife said to me, "If I have to eat one more dish of schnitzel…" That's when I recalled that here at home I ate Mexican, Italian, Japanese, and Greek food all in the same week, not to mention the double cheeseburger and fries—you have to have some American food, right?

We human beings are the absolutely unique creature that God made, for He made us in His own image and likeness, and the diets the Lord gave us in the Garden, and after the Flood, are clearly intended to both sustain us and to differentiate us from all other living creatures, to identify us as human and not animal. Israel was created by the Lord to be His own particular possession among all the peoples of the earth, and so the Lord gave Israel a diet that would sustain and identify Israel as His own people. And this, of course, is not unknown, for all the religions and all the idols prescribe diets and prohibit certain foods. There are many dietary prohibitions in Mormonism, Hinduism, Islam, and virtually every religion that I can think of, all for the purpose of creating communal and spiritual identity.

The really interesting thing is, no such prohibitions exist for us. And this has been somewhat of a problem. We Christians have off and on suffered from what I call Dietary Prohibition Envy; and we have wanted to have a diet like other religions have where we're not supposed to eat certain things, so that we can be known by those prohibitions because it's in the prohibition that the identity is discovered in other religions. And the Lord didn't prohibit us from eating anything.

And so it was that we have yearned for those prohibitions and sometimes invented them. I remember when I was a young person—those of us over fifty might all remember—when our Roman Catholic friends and neighbors couldn't eat meat on Friday, right? So at my public school in the cafeteria, there was always fish for the Roman Catholic students. We all knew who they were because they were eating that fish, right? And it was a marker, not of Christian identity, but certainly of Roman Catholic identity.

And while Protestants often scoffed at this, Protestants, also longing for a diet that would identify them, often embraced teetotalerism. About the same time that the Roman Catholics gave up the Friday fast from meat, Methodists gave up official institutional teetotalerism. You know, up until the late sixties, Methodist clergy had to sign the pledge that liquor would never touch their lips, and anyone serving on a governing board of a Methodist congregation also had to take the pledge. That was abandoned in the late sixties although it has not been abandoned completely ever in Protestantism. I remember once about thirty-five years ago, looking through a temperance hymnal (I wish I had it). What I remember was the immortal hymn,

> I won't drink, smoke, or chew,
> or go around with those who do.

How could a good book like that have gotten away from me? I don't know.

The Seventh-day Adventists, a Christian sect, have gone all the way; and if the Roman Catholics and the Methodists finally abandoned their dietary prohibition, the Seventh-day Adventists embraced it. They have a sacred diet; they are vegetarians: meat is prohibited to them and it is certainly a marker of Seventh-day Adventists' identity. Of course, it has nothing to do with Christianity.

I also want to point out that in our increasingly godless and re-paganizing society, we are looking for dietary prohibitions because, you see, while we may be abandoning Christianity and our Lord Jesus Christ and western civilization, we need something to fill the vacuum. And so we are abounding in the old religions and the new ones coming back, and diet has become a big thing. I don't know if you've noticed that, but I certainly have. Christian civilizations celebrated food in all its forms, but the post-Christian culture of today constantly warns us about the dangers of the food we eat; we've become obsessed with food. Several years ago I attended a reception at a university and I was wandering in the faculty lounge trying to enjoy my wine and cheese, and as I put a piece of cheddar cheese into my mouth, a faculty member kind of sidled up to me and said, "You know, eating that stuff is like injecting poison straight into your vein." Really! You can't make these things up.

And in case you haven't heard, a group calling itself The Cancer Project has just filed a lawsuit against the makers of hot dogs; they're demanding a warning label that informs us that hot dogs and other processed meat increase the risk of cancer. We are becoming food-phobic. 'Don't eat it! It's bad for you.' All those things around my elementary school classroom that I was exhorted to eat so I would be strong and healthy, I learn now are poison. Right? This is true.

In my childhood, food was a good thing; today everything is a threat. And I believe that that is part of the neopagan desire to control our diet and to enforce their prohibitions and to form us as modern people, no longer Christian, but embracing the religion of What's Happening Now.

In Christ, there are no dietary prohibitions, but there is a Christian diet. Our Lord Jesus Christ gives Himself to be our food.

> I am the living bread, which came down from heaven;
> if anyone eats of this bread, he will live forever, and the
> bread which I shall give for the life of the world is my
> flesh. (Jn 6:51)

Or, as He shall say to us this morning,

> Take and eat; this is My body, which is given for you.

This diet gives us life, the life we all desire, unending life with God; it unites us with the Lord and with one another and therefore creates our identity, not through prohibition but through union with the Lord and with one another in Him. It is the source of all true festivity for in the Eucharist our bread becomes the body of Christ and the body of Christ becomes our bread, and he who eats this bread shall live forever. This diet comes with no warning labels or prohibitions because it is the fulfillment of all diets sacred and pseudo-sacred, promising the fullness of life in time and eternity.

> Taste and see that the Lord is good;
> blessed are those who trust in Him. (Ps 34:8)

Amen.

9

I Want to Live Forever

In the name of the Father, and of the Son,
and of the Holy Spirit.

I want to live forever, and I pray that you do, too.

When I was thirty, I had a parishioner named James Kirk, sixty-four years my senior. I always called him *Mister* Kirk. Mr. Kirk had been diagnosed with leukemia when he was eighty-four years old. On Easter Sunday of his ninety-fourth year, having struggled against his illness for a decade, he came to church wearing a really beautiful new suit. And when I greeted him at the door, I commented on it. And I can still see him to this day stroking the lapel as he said to me, "I ought to get a few good years out of this!" And he did! He did.

It's often said that the young think they're immortal, and there's truth in that, but in a very restricted sense. When I was young, I understood that someday I would die, and at the same time I thought I'd live forever. And what I mean by that apparent contradiction is this: that when I was fifteen, I thought that the length of time that it would take to get from being fifteen to the age I am now was equivalent to forever. I'm certain that Kenny's over there—listening I hope!—and thinking it's true, right? Forever is the length of time it's going to take him to get from there [where he is] to here [where I am]. But of course, as all of us who've reached middle age or beyond know, the years go by just like that.

I want to live forever, and I pray that you do too, because God created us to live forever. God did not create us to live for a brief time and then perish; He created us to live forever. And therefore, by nature I want to live forever, and that's why I hope that you do, too, because you are created to live forever.

In today's reading from the Gospel of St. Luke, our Lord is questioned by some Sadducees. Their purpose was not to learn from the Lord, neither was it to determine what it was that He believed and taught, but to make Him look foolish and discredit Him. The Sadducees were primarily aristocrats whose piety centered on the Temple in Jerusalem, its priesthood, and the Torah, the first five books of the Bible.[1] And while it may come as some surprise, we need to under-

---

[1] Indeed, it was thought for a long time that the Saducees only considered the books of Moses, the first five books of the Bible, to be inspired scripture; we now think that

stand that in the covenant that God made with Abraham and with Moses and Israel, God does not promise anyone eternal life. While the prophets and Moses certainly tell us that we have souls, we are not told that they are immortal. There is no life after death for ancient Israel. And so it is that the Psalmist writes this:

> The dead do not praise the Lord,
>> nor do any that go down into the silence.

That's Psalm 115. Psalm 88 puts it this way.

> I am a man who has no strength,
> like one forsaken among the dead,
>> like the slain that lie in the grave,
> like those whom Thou, O Lord,
>>> dost remember no more,
>> for they are cut off from Thy hand.

For early Israel, the sphere of relationship with God and with the neighbor, was this life and this world and they expected no other. Slowly over the centuries, the Lord began to reveal through the prophets that there could be a resurrection from the dead. But it was not an explicit promise; it was implied, suggested. And slowly there came to be those

---

may not quite be true, but certainly for them, the first five books of the Bible were the authoritative books.

among the Israelites who became convinced that the Lord was promising a resurrection from the dead, at least for the Israelites.

But for the Sadducees, this was not so. They were of the party of those Israelites who rejected this belief, not finding it in the books of Moses. Therefore, in order to mock the Lord, they raised a question that arises from Mosaic law.

In Deuteronomy, the twenty-fifth chapter, we read this. "If brothers dwell together and one of them dies and has no son, the wife of the dead shall not be married outside of the family to a stranger. Her husband's brother shall go in to her and take her as his wife and perform the duty of a husband's brother to her." This is known as the Levirite Law, from the Latin *levir*, a husband's brother, or brother-in-law. And so the Sadducees ask a question concerning the woman who enters into a Levirite marriage seven times. (Lk 20:33) "Whose wife," they ask, "will she be in the resurrection?" They ask that mockingly.

The Lord's answer is simple and direct. (Lk 20:34-36) In the Resurrection, we will neither marry nor be given in marriage. Marriage is instituted by God for this world and for this life—marriage and the generation of children. Christian marriage vows therefore, are made until death parts us. This is why a Christian widow or widower can remarry without becoming either an adulterer or a polygamist. But the Lord adds something that can be easily misunderstood. He tells the Sadducees and us that in the Resurrection we

77

will be equal to angels. By this the Lord does not mean that we will be disembodied spirits, which is what angels are, for the whole point of resurrection is that we will be embodied spirits, just as we are now.

Marriage and the generation of children is for this life and for this world, but in the Kingdom of God we, the children of God, shall be fruitful in another way. And then, just as the Sadducees' question was drawn from the books of Moses, whose teaching was for them authoritative, the Lord responds by referring to the books of Moses, to the book of Exodus. The Lord tells them that even Moses affirmed the Resurrection in his account of the burning bush. (Lk 20:37-38)

During the Jewish war against the Romans of AD 66-70, the Sadducees, along with the Temple of Jerusalem and it's priesthood, all disappeared, it all disappeared from history. The leadership of Judaism passed to the Pharisees who, like the Sadducees, opposed Jesus but, unlike them, believed in a future resurrection. There are no known Sadducees among the early disciples of our Lord, but there certainly were Pharisees who became disciples of our Lord and the most important of them without question is the apostle Paul, who used this disagreement between the Pharisees and the Sadducees to save his own life. (There's no time to go into that but if you want to make a note, you can read all about it in the 23rd chapter of the Acts of the Apostles.)

℃

We believe in the resurrection of the dead and the life of the world to come, not because we agree with the Pharisees against the Sadducees, but because our Lord Jesus Christ said, "I am the Resurrection and the Life," (Jn 11:25) and then proved that when He was raised from the dead and appeared to His disciples bodily. Apart from His resurrection and His bodily appearance, all talk of resurrection is purely speculative. I want to live forever, and the Lord has promised me that I will if I share in His resurrection and eternal life.

I will not live forever in this world and that's a very good thing. The great Asian religions do not teach resurrection but reincarnation. The great Asian religions teach that we are born, live, die and are reborn, live, die and are reborn endlessly. And the purpose of Buddhism, for instance, is to release the person from the crushing wheel of death and rebirth. If our Lord is Who He says He is and His words are true, then no one is reincarnated, but the Asian religions have intuited spiritually a great truth with their doctrine of reincarnation, and it is this: that to live on and on endlessly forever in this world is hell. That's exactly what their doctrine means.

Life is good. Life is good because God is good, and I want to live forever, but I do not want to live forever in this world or anywhere else. I only want to live forever if I can live forever in the good God, the Father, the Son, and the Holy Spirit.

Amen.

10

The Goal of Every Journey

In the name of the Father, and of the Son,
and of the Holy Spirit.

Being called upon to have political opinions seems to me to
be part of the price of living in a democracy, so every now
and then someone plagues me with questions about poli-
tics: am I a Democrat or a Republican? a liberal or a con-
servative? a capitalist or a socialist? I used to avoid these
questions but I've come slowly to welcome them because
they give me an opportunity to reveal that I am 'none of
the above.' I am a monarchist! [*Applause*] Of course, when
I say that, people do tend to laugh. They don't always ap-
plaud but they laugh. And when they find out that I'm serious, people are often scandalized; they believe—errone-
ously—that I want America to renounce democracy and
embrace royalty, and of course nothing could be further
from the truth.

I'm a native-born American, cherish my citizenship, always try to fulfill my civic responsibilities, have never failed to vote in an election. And I also love my country and never so much as when I'm not in it. To travel outside the United States means to know that there is no place on earth like this place. And this is known, of course, by untold millions of people around the world. Over twenty years ago, I was in London; the London Times magazine had a cover article claiming that two-thirds of all the immigration in the entire world was to the United States. I'm sure that not much has changed since then except perhaps an increasing percentage. A week or so ago I was watching a documentary about a great cargo ship transporting automobiles from Europe to the United States, and the crew had to go through all of the cars and all of the ship looking for stowaways because, as the documentary said, "for those people seeking the fabled 'better life,' America is the holy grail."

Except for an occasional afternoon in Tijuana, and a couple trips to Canada, I had never been able to travel outside the United States to go to any of those places that I'd been reading about all my life until, in 1988, my parishioners blessed me with a two month sabbatical so that I could go on pilgrimage, and that sabbatical was to be followed by a month's vacation to be spent with my family. I took the trip of a lifetime. By the way, 1988—some of you may not remember 1988! Well, it was a dark age. No cellphones! No internet cafes, you know? Where you could email people.

And when I flew out of New York for London, I realized I was on my own, and nobody would be hearing from me, and I wouldn't be hearing from them, for a long time. I wandered through England, much of Europe, and finally arrived at what I thought was my destination and goal, Jerusalem.

It was all wonderful, it really was. I saw the sacred places and met wonderful people. But we live in a fallen world and like all of life in this world, there was a downside. For example, I was robbed in Madrid, and the thieves got my plane tickets. I wandered through three countries over several days trying to get them replaced. It was an adventure all in itself. Then, a week or two later in Munich, Germany, I went into the bank to get a cash advance on my credit card. And while I stood there waiting for my money, I saw Frau Peschel (I shall always remember her name.) hold up my credit card (She was behind glass.) smile at me and as she looked me in the eye, she took shears and cut my credit card in two. It was a shocking experience. Turned out that the one phone call back home I'd been able to make was to my travel agent in the process of trying to get my tickets replaced, and the travel agent called my wife, my wife thought my credit card had been stolen, she cancelled it. Well! It was a shock. Then, having finally arrived in Israel, I tried to leave the country but, when I got to the airport in Tel Aviv, the authorities were waiting for me, and they put me through a three-hour interrogation, groups of revolving interrogators asking me the same questions all the time and over and over again, finally ending with a strip search immediately before they allowed me to leave the country. That was an experience, believe me. By the way, it seems that the big problem was that I had spent a lot of time that week with Palestinian Christians and I was traveling all alone, and that made me suspect.

In any event, in the end I learned a great lesson, a great truth. It wasn't what I expected to learn; it was more than what I had expected to learn. I learned that the goal, the destination of my journey was not Jerusalem, but home. I learned that having a home and expecting to get there is what makes a trip good, even when it's difficult. I was a pilgrim, and I wandered through and prayed in village churches and great cathedrals, Canterbury, Notre Dame de Paris, St. Peter's, to name just a few. And every day that I was in Israel, in Jerusalem, I prayed in the Church of the Holy Sepulchre. But all along the way, I protected my passport even more carefully than my money. And I knew that Dorothy, our children, my parents, my sister and her family, and a world of friends were waiting for me and would want to hear the story of all my adventures. It was home, I realized, that made my journey a good and joyful thing. And I believe that that's true for our journey through life.

In today's Gospel, our beloved brother and Lord tells Pilate and us that He is a King. (Jn 18:37) He had always refused to be made King and you may remember that after the feeding of the five thousand, when they tried to take Him by force and make Him King, He slipped away; and whenever people tried to apply that title to Him, He also deflected it. But now as He approaches His crucifixion, He can and must reveal Himself for Who He is, the origin and goal of all that is. Pilate will fail to comprehend what our Lord is talking about. And the Jews will reject Him, but that no longer matters. He is a King and He has come to bear witness to the truth, and the truth is the Father's love for the world which the Son manifests in His life, death, and resurrection.

Our Lord said that He was the good shepherd, who would lay down His life for His sheep. (Jn 10:11) Now when we hear that, we think of shepherds and sheep. But any Israelite at the time of our Lord, who heard that, knew that He was saying, "I am the good King, the King Who will lay down His life for His subjects." And so it is that He would be enthroned on the cross, crowned with thorns and, unwittingly, Pilate would proclaim the truth of the Lord's identity on the *titulus* above His head in Hebrew, Latin, and Greek. Our Lord is a King but He tells the fearful and uncomprehending Pilate that His Kingship is neither of or from this world, and He also tells Pilate and reminds us, that this is a fallen world, when He says that if His Kingdom were of this world, His disciples would fight.

In a fallen world, nations and peoples exist only so long as they can defend themselves by force of arms. In my travels, I discovered something that amazed me over twenty years ago, but no more. I discovered that tiny Switzerland—neutral for centuries, the land of mountain meadows, cowbells, alphorn players, (right?)—is armed to the teeth. It really is. Their army and air force are constantly on maneuvers. I think all the citizens of the citizens' army have automatic weapons under their beds at home. And all of the tunnels and mountain passes into the country are mined so that they can be blown up quickly sealing the country from invaders by land. When Israel was formed, modern Israel, just a few decades ago, they did not model their military, their army, after the great superpowers; Israel modeled its army after the army of Switzerland.

To live in this world for any length of time is to learn that security is always fragile and peace always temporary. The Kingdom of Christ our Lord is not in this world or of this world, it is beyond this world. And we Christians are all pilgrims traveling through this world to our true home. In the words of the Letter to the Hebrews,

> Here we have no lasting city, but we seek the city
> which is to come. (Heb 13:14)

But if we are not yet home, Christ is just as much our King now in this world as He will be then, and we owe Him our absolute allegiance today, just as we will in the endless day of His eternal Kingdom.

Like nations, earthly leaders of whatever description or competence come and go, but we have a King Who lives forever and a homeland that is imperishable. And so it is that I really am a monarchist; I have a King. And if you believe and are baptized, so do you. I guard my baptismal certificate and what it represents, as I journey through this fallen world even more carefully than I guard my passport when I travel through foreign lands. Life in this world can be, and often is, a good and joyful thing, and I'm certainly enjoying my journey and I pray that you are enjoying yours. Our King is leading us home and He will welcome us when we arrive. He has promised us a place in His Father's house and there we will praise Him forever, Jesus Christ, the King of endless glory.

And there are times when I wonder if, when I arrive, He and all those He has gathered to Himself, I wonder if they'll want to hear about all my adventures, the way my family did when I arrived home in 1988. I hope so, because I have stories to tell. But of course, I've been telling the Lord those stories every day.

Amen.

PART III

The Mystery of Holiness

11

Be Prepared

In the name of the Father, and of the Son,
and of the Holy Spirit.

A week and a half ago, Dorothy and I were just getting ready to go in to have cream tea at a beautiful inn on Cape Cod when my phone rang. It was Father Doran. He felt so guilty for having called me on vacation, that he offered to preach for me last Sunday, which I really appreciated since we got back late and I certainly didn't want to. However I begin by telling you that because three weeks ago I began a meditation on the mystery of holiness, in preparation for All Saints. And that meditation has gone on. And it's a recurring reflection over years and years and years.

The saints are nothing if not exemplary Christians: men and women that we are to imitate and not simply admire or marvel at, even though they are incredible in many ways and the more you get to know about them the more amazing they become. Nevertheless, the church has always held them up for us because we're meant to, in some way, imitate them. And the apostle Paul put the matter bluntly— he was certainly a very great saint—when he wrote to the Corinthians,

Be imitators of me, as I am of Christ. (1Cor 11:1)

The word 'saint' comes from the Latin word 'sanctus,' which means holy. And we are to imitate the saints as they the Christ Who was the Holy One of God. And that's what we always have to remember, that there really is only One Who is holy, and that's God.

You know, our Lord had a lot of His disciples desert Him during His ministry, and at one point He said to the apostles and to others, "Are you going to leave me as well?" And the apostle Peter, answering for the others, said,

Lord, to whom shall we go? You have the words of eternal life. And we have believed and have come to know that You are the Holy One of God. (Jn 6:68)

And the demons also recognized Him, and they said to Him,

We know Who You are. You are the Holy One of God. (Lk 4:34)

And so it is that all holiness is derivative from the Holy One, God the Son, our Lord Jesus Christ. The saints are exemplary. They are to be imitated. And they imitate Christ. But the question I've been pondering (for decades it seems) is... exactly what are we supposed to imitate?

St. Paul traveled around on great missionary journeys, but I don't think I'm supposed to do that. St. Benedict Joseph Labré was a beggar in Rome. St. Louis, after whom the city is named, was the King of France. Just think of the difference between those two saints! St. Anthony the Great of the Desert—one of my favorite saints. (I've had his icon on my wall for thirty-five years.) St. Anthony the Great of the Desert went out, prayed and fasted for decades and became one of the most influential men of his time, and his influence has gone on and will go on until the Lord does return. He is the father of monks, an Egyptian peasant who was illiterate. One of the most literate men who ever lived— St. Thomas Aquinas—lived nine hundred years later and wrote books that will always be read as long as there are people who think, Christians or non-Christians. And while St. Anthony the Great of the Desert fasted for decades, St. Thomas Aquinas ate so much they had to make a special desk for him, to accommodate his great girth.

Now I wonder who I am to imitate. Which one of them, in their dietary habits, are to be my model? And of course, that's just the point. I'm not supposed to imitate these things. I'm not called to be a beggar or a king or an illiterate peasant fasting in the wilderness or a great theologian, and I don't think any of you are either. So what is it that they imitate in the Lord that we also are to imitate?

I'm asking these questions because I believe they are directly relevant to the Word of God for us today. Our Lord tells us to be ready for His final and glorious appearing. In the Nicene Creed we say, "He shall come again in glory to judge the quick and the dead," and establish His glorious Kingdom. That's what we are to be prepared for and He says it could come at any time, day or night. It will come at a time we do not expect.

> Watch, therefore, for you know neither the day nor the hour. (Mt 25:13)

And so we're supposed to be ready, in a kind of active waiting, for the Lord to appear. So that we are like the wise virgins who rejoice at His appearing.

And so I come back to the question. What is it about the Lord and His exemplary brothers and sisters that each and every one of us who are baptized into Him, and who are therefore holy, are to imitate? The answer, I am convinced, is this: our Lord Jesus Christ is humble and grateful. That's what characterizes Him in all His words and in all His deeds, His humility and His gratitude. And that's what all the saints have in common with Him and with one another in spite of all their radical diversity, and that's what each and every one of us baptized into Him is supposed to share with Him and with them. The apostle Paul wrote to the Thessalonians,

> Rejoice always. Pray constantly. Give thanks in all circumstances. For this is the will of God in Christ Jesus for you. (1Thess 5:16-18)

And I like to remember that, and I repeat that verse often, because I have a lot of trouble remembering what the will of God is for me. How often I wonder, "What is the will of God for me?" As if it's some great mystery! And then I remember: rejoice always, pray constantly, give thanks in all circumstances. There it is. I know what the will of God is for me. But when the apostle Paul says, 'Give thanks in all circumstances,' he's asking us to imitate the Lord, "Who, in the night in which He was betrayed," to be handed over to sinful men who would do terrible things to Him and kill him, "gave thanks."

We hear that every mass. "On the night in which he was betrayed, He took bread and gave thanks." Our Lord is always and everywhere thankful to the Father Who sent Him. His gratitude is not oriented toward the world where circumstances are always changing, but rather has God the Father as its object.

After that final meal when He gave thanks to the Father, He went out into the garden of Gethsemane and He prayed,

> My Father, if it be possible, let this cup pass from Me, nevertheless, not as I will but as You will. (Mt 26:39)

And a little later He added,

> My Father, if this cannot pass unless I drink it, Your will be done. (Mt 26:42)

With these words and the deeds that followed them, the Lord manifested His perfect humility. Years afterward, in his Letter to the Philippians, St. Paul wrote of our Lord, "He humbled Himself and became obedient unto death, even death on a cross." (Phil 2:8) In Eastern Orthodox churches, they have an icon of the Lord in the repose of death, and the title of the icon is, "Extreme Humility."

> He humbled himself and became obedient unto death, even death on a cross.

Our Lord's gratitude is independent of circumstances because it has the Father as its object, and the Lord's humility is His willing subordination to the will of the Father. That's humility. Humility isn't saying, "Oh gosh, I'm not really very good at that." Humility means subordinating my will to the will of God, ordering my will *under* His will, *sub*-ordinating. And our Lord Jesus Christ is the model of that willing subordination. He said to His detractors at one point,

> I can do nothing on my own authority. As I hear, I judge. And my judgment is just because I seek not My Own will, but the will of Him Who sent Me. (Jn 5:30)

And that is the humility of the Christ, and that's what the saints have in common with Him, what they share in Him. And it's a sign of their holiness.

Our Lord warns us that He's coming at an hour that we do not expect and to be ready, as are the wise virgins in the parable. (Mt 25:1-13) This means praying always for the gifts of gratitude and humility and exercising these gifts in imitation of the Lord. The church is called to be a community of gratitude and humility. That's really what we're all called to be: grateful and humble before the Lord.

In just a few minutes, I will pray on behalf of all of us, "It is very meet, right, and our bounden duty that we should at all times and in all places give thanks unto Thee, O Lord, Holy Father, Almighty, Everlasting God."

This gratitude, which the faithful have acknowledged as a duty throughout the ages, is one with the humility that puts the will of our Father before our own. To live each day with gratitude and humility is to be ready at all times and in all places for the appearing of the Bridegroom, our Lord Jesus Christ, and to be truly prepared to celebrate with Him the Marriage Feast which has no end.

Amen.

12

The Most Vertical Man

In the name of the Father, the Son, and the
Holy Spirit.

A few years ago, Dorothy and I drove through Nova Scotia in mid-October. The weather was clear and everywhere we looked we saw a blaze of reds, oranges, and yellows. The landscape was as beautiful as we had hoped it would be when we left the palm trees and Mediterranean sky of San Diego. But I saw more than the trees when I got there. In the midst of all the color and beauty of Nova Scotia, we saw churches—not an exceptional thing to see—but these churches were almost always white, and they had steeples that pierced the sky, reaching up above the trees, pointing beyond the creation to the Creator. All over the province we saw them: mostly Anglican, mostly made of white wood, possessed of a striking verticality. They were simple, but they gave to that beautiful landscape what it really could never give to itself. They gave meaning. The spires of those churches pointing to heaven were a reminder that all the beauty of the world comes from God, Who made it and sustains it. Or, to put it another way: without God, trees are merely a wilderness and each tree in it one more earth-bound creature passing away.

After a couple days in the southern part of the province and Halifax, the major city, we traveled north to Cape Breton Isle, to the city of Sydney where we were staying, as we wanted to go to the the Cabot Trail which is very famous and very beautiful. And Sydney is not beautiful, but two blocks from our hotel, there was one of these beautiful churches, very simple on the exterior, with a great steeple piercing the sky. We went to Mass on Sunday morning, and when we entered, we discovered a church that possessed even greater verticality inside than outside. It was very beautiful, Gothic, with white walls and high vaulted arches with gold ribs. And it lifted me up. The Mass and the sermon, I'm sorry to say, were as flat as a pancake; but the building rescued everything. It was a silent proclamation of the glory of God and of the faith of the people who had built it. It was just wonderful. And when the priest said, "Lift up your hearts," I could say, "We lift them up to the Lord," and really mean it in that wonderful place.

We call this building and all buildings like it the church,

but of course it's not the church. The word 'church' comes from the Greek *ekklesia* which means 'assembly.' It is the assembly of the faithful, to do the things we are doing right now, that is the church. We are the church. The building itself is a symbol of ourselves, it is a representation in wood and plaster and stone and glass of ourselves. And the question isn't so much, "Does the building possess architectural verticality?" but "Do we?" That's the question.

As I never tire of pointing out, (and therefore you may have been around when I have been pointing it out on other occasions) we human beings are the vertical creatures in the world. All the animals of the earth, great and small, have spines that are horizontal, that are parallel to the earth, while man alone stands upright. And this expresses a spiritual reality, a reality that we need to be able to read. The Lord God made all the animals along with everything else in His creation for us. But He made us for Himself. And He placed us in the world to be signs pointing heavenward, to Him. And that's part of what it means to be created in the divine image and likeness, and to have dominion.

I have a wonderful dog: Sebastian, my greyhound. He's a sweet gentle creature, and he only looks up to me. He has that horizontal spine running parallel to the earth, and he's a reminder all the time of the world that God made for us. But I am to stand upright and to point beyond this world. Of course it's possible to stand upright, to be erect, without being upright, isn't it? When we say someone is upright or upstanding, we're talking about a quality of the person. Our language expresses a truth, that an upright person is good. And as our Lord tells us, all goodness comes from God alone. And the upright person is a sign of the good God. We say likewise of the dishonest or morally corrupt person that he is bent, crooked, or low.

Buildings can reach high into the sky but not point upward. In our world the great buildings are commercial skyscrapers and they dwarf all the churches in our cities. You may have seen a picture of St. Patrick's cathedral sitting there now, surrounded by these buildings towering over it. But the commercial skyscraper does not point upward. It is a symbol of the power of money and therefore, for all its greatness and grandeur, it is as earthbound as the proverbial lead balloon.

When man fell and lost the knowledge of God, the Lord God created a people for Himself, Israel, to be a vertical nation, one that pointed to Him, the Lord and God Who had made all the peoples and nations of the earth. And Israel was to be that nation that was pointing to God, calling all the other nations and peoples away from their idolatry and to Him. The Lord God said through the prophet Isaiah,

> I have made you (Israel) a light to the nations so that
> my salvation might reach to the ends of the earth.
> (Is 49:6)

When the Israelites forgot the Lord and themselves fell into idolatry, the Lord sent them prophets—that is, messengers—to remind them of who and what He had created them and called them to be. The last of those prophets of ancient Israel was St. John the Baptist, the most vertical, the most upright of men who ever lived. The Lord called him the greatest man born of woman. John apparently had great personal appeal, what we now call charisma, was greatly admired and had many disciples devoted to him. But when asked about himself, whether or not he were the Christ—that is, the anointed one of God who would rescue Israel—or Elijah, the prophet who had not died, (You know, Elijah was taken off into heaven in a fiery chariot and the Israelites believed that he would return immediately before the Messiah.) or, they asked, are you the Prophet?—the mysterious prophet that Moses mentioned in the Book of Deuteronomy—John said, "I am not." (Jn 1:21)

When asked why he was baptizing, if not the Christ or Elijah or the Prophet, he would only say as we just heard in the Gospel, "I baptize with water but among you stands One Whom you do not know, even He Who comes after me, the thong of whose sandals I am not worthy to untie." (Jn 1:26) And here I really do need to point out that John the Baptist did not administer the sacrament of Christian baptism. The baptism we have received is not the baptism that he administered. John pointed away from himself to an Other. He was the messenger but not the message. He was a

sign in flesh and blood of an Other, the One Who had created him and Who sent him to speak and to baptize.

Like John, we are to point beyond ourselves to the One Who
is ever present yet coming. John lived immediately before
the first advent of our Lord while we await His final advent.
And like John, we are called to be living reminders in flesh
and blood of the Lord's presence and of His promised coming again to judge the world in righteousness.

The world is ever and always in flight from its creator
and redeemer. The apostle Paul points out in the first chapter of Romans that we human beings seem always more
ready to worship the creature than we are the creator. We see
this every December in the progressive purging of Christmas from our public life. Every December it gets worse (or
better, depending on your beliefs). We are exhorted now to
send holiday cards, buy and give holiday gifts, eat holiday
meals, erect holiday trees, and go to Balboa Park, certainly
not to celebrate 'Christmas on the Prado,' but rather, 'December Nights.'

The world wants the holiday without the Holy One; it
wants the gift without the Giver. It would like to forget the
Creator. And God has called us to share in His life, to be a
vertical people, to be like John the Baptist, to be like those
churches with their great spires, to point the world beyond
the world, to direct the world's attention beyond itself to

the One Who created it and Who has promised to come in glory to make a new heaven and a new earth.

Amen.

13

The Cost of Discipleship

In the name of the Father and of the Son
and of the Holy Spirit.

I want to tell you the stories of two women, one known to me in life and the other in literature. The first one was a visitor to my church twenty years ago. She appeared at the Sunday morning Eucharist; she was very well dressed and she was very attentive, and she was very Japanese. And she returned the next week and the week after that and she was at the Eucharist every Sunday for a couple of months, and finally she left me a visitors card with her name, address, and phone number, which I took as an invitation to call, which I did. And she invited me to her home to speak with her and to meet her husband. And I said, well, I'd love to visit and when could we arrange that? And she said, well, it would have to be after ten pm some evening, because my husband is an executive with a Japanese electronics firm here on a very short visa, working on Torrey Pines Road and he never gets home before ten pm. So on a Tuesday evening, at 10:30 at night, I dragged myself out of the house and over to their apartment. And as I stepped in, she shrieked, and I realized that I had to take my shoes off! And when I got inside, I realized there was no furniture. And we had to sit on the floor and drink tea. I guess this is where multiculturalism comes home! In any event, I spoke for awhile with her husband, a very interesting man, and then she told me her story. And her story was a simple one.

She had a friend in Japan, a close friend, who was a Christian, and her friend had shared her faith with her, had told her about our Lord Jesus Christ, and had shared the meaning of her faith. And this woman was drawn to our Lord and drawn to Christianity, but she told me that she could never attend church in Japan. She was able to come to church every Sunday in the States because no one knew her and because her husband gave his permission. She said, "In Japan, if I were ever to be baptized and go to church, or even just go to church as I am going now, I would be shunned by my family and by my friends because only one percent of the Japanese are Christian, and Japan is ruled by the group." And as she told me her story, all I could think of was the gospel that we just heard read.[1]

---

[1] [Transcriber's Footnote:] Now great multitudes accompanied Him; and He turned and said to them, "If anyone comes to me and does not hate his own father and mother and wife and children and brothers and sisters, yes, and even his own life, he cannot be my disciple. Whoever does not bear his own cross and come after me, cannot be

And every time I hear this gospel read in the Liturgy or any time I read it apart from the Liturgy, I think of my Japanese visitor who had counted the cost of discipleship and knew that she could not and would not pay that cost.

The second woman I want to tell you about is one known to me from literature, from her autobiography *A Memory for Wonders*. She was born in France before the Second World War, and her parents were ardent communists and zealous atheists to the point where they left France and moved to Morocco (this was in the days of the French Empire in North Africa). And they moved to Morocco in part so that, and I quote from her autobiography, "in order that no one would speak to her of God (by which they meant the Holy Trinity) and influence the development of her mind with oppressive superstition." But God is always at work no matter what. And this girl, Lucette Le Goulard, at a very early age, looking at the beauty of the landscape in which she lived, became convinced that there must be One Who had made it, that there must be a Creator. And she became convinced

---

my disciple. For which of you, desiring to build a tower, does not first sit down and count the cost, whether he has enough to complete it? Otherwise, when he has laid a foundation, and is not able to finish, all who see it begin to mock him, saying, 'This man began to build, and was not able to finish.' Or what king, going to encounter another king in war, will not sit down first and take counsel whether he is able with ten thousand to meet him who comes against him with twenty thousand? And if not, while the other is yet a great way off, he sends an embassy and asks terms of peace. So therefore, whoever of you does not renounce all that he cannot be my disciple." (Lk 14:25-33)

of that, and as she grew older, she began—of course, without her parents' knowledge—to go into churches and there she sat before the Eucharistic Presence of our Lord and in the silence of the churches, she heard Him calling her. And eventually, she was instructed in the faith, and baptized and told her parents, and her father physically attacked her in a terrible rage, beating her with his fists so violently that he broke her glasses and the lens of her glasses, and her eye was cut. And after that vicious beating, he and his wife disowned their daughter Lucette, telling her that they never wanted to see her again, that she was not their daughter. And she had expected this, perhaps she didn't expect to be beaten, but she knew that her parents would be violently opposed, and she went on to join the Poor Clares, became a contemplative nun, founded two flourishing convents of Poor Clare nuns in North Africa. She also had heard our Lord call her. She had considered the cost of discipleship, and she was willing to pay that cost.

The stories I've just told illustrate the meaning of our Lord's words but I'm fairly certain that few of us come from situations like the situations I've just described. Quite the contrary. Most of us come from families that have not been an obstacle to our faith, but a means of faith, like Riley, our baptismal candidate this morning. Or like my grandson, my wonderful new grandson, that I expect to baptize here at St. Michael's next Sunday. Many if not most of us were brought to the Church, as Riley has been brought to the Church, as an infant or small child, to receive the grace of baptism and become an adopted child of God, because our parents believed and wanted to share their faith with us and prayed that we would become sharers in their faith and disciples of our Lord Jesus Christ.

Now this isn't true for all of us. There are those of us here who were baptized as adults, people who were not brought by Christian families into the Church, but even then, I rarely, if ever, hear a story of anyone whose family has utterly disowned them because of their faith.

So what is the Lord Jesus Christ saying to us, those of us who do not have to overcome great obstacles but have been surrounded by people who prayed for us and encouraged us and hoped that we would be faithful to our Lord Jesus Christ?

Well, the first thing is, our Lord is proclaiming His identity in the words we heard in today's Gospel, for only the Lord God has the right to make such a demand on us, the demand that the Lord makes on us in today's Gospel. If anyone else makes that demand, you know they're evil. Only God has a right to make such a demand. He's reminding us in uncompromising language of the meaning of the first of the ten commandments, "You shall have no other gods," (Ex 20:3) and its amplification found in the book of Deuteronomy, "You shall love the Lord your God with all your heart, with all your mind, with all your soul, and with all your strength." (Deut 6:5) And our Lord Jesus Christ Himself said this is the greatest commandment in the Law.

Nothing, not even those we love most and those who love us most, is to compete with God, and Jesus is God the Son, the visibility of God the Father both in time and eternity, having said to His disciples and to every one of us, "If you have seen Me, you have seen the Father; I and the Father are One." (Jn 14:9, 10:30)

Therefore, to follow our Lord Jesus Christ as God and Man, means to renounce everything, as our Lord says in the Gospel. But what in the world does that mean?

Well, here I can only share with you what I've come to understand after decades of reflection, study, and most of all, prayer. This is what I believe it means to renounce everything for the Lord. In the beginning of his letter, the apostle James wrote this:

> Every good endowment and every perfect gift, is from above, coming down from the Father of Lights with Whom there is no variation or shadow due to change. (Jas 1:17)

At the heart of our Christian faith is the knowledge that every good thing comes from God. He is the Giver of every good gift and we are to never love the gift more than the Giver. Let me say that again, because that's the heart of the matter. We are never to love the gift more than the Giver.

To love the gift more than the God Who gives it, is the very definition of idolatry. My children are certainly among the very best gifts that God has given to me, and I love them more than my own life, quite literally. But if I love them more than the God Who has given them to me, I make them into gods. I literally do what we popularly say: I 'idolize' them. Right? Well, what is it to idolize someone except to make that person into a god or goddess, to put that person in the place of god? And this is hazardous and destructive, both to the person idolized, or the thing idolized, and to the person who idolizes. To see my children as people to be loved but not idolized means to see them as a gift of our Lord and never allow them to come between me and the Lord Who made them. To idolize someone means to enter into illusion, for the creature is not the Creator. And to recognize and live this is to make the necessary renunciation that our Lord is speaking of in today's Gospel. He's not asking us to make this renunciation for His sake. He's asking us to make it for our sake.

And now I'll tell you the rest of the story of Lucette Le Goulard, who became Mother Veronica Namoyo Le Goulard, and who founded those monasteries of contemplative women in North Africa. The last thing I know of her from her autobiography is that she went to Lusaka, Zambia, to revive a dying convent of Poor Clare nuns and to restore it to health. And, mysteriously—since God is always at work, as I said at the beginning—decades after her family's break with her, her parents heard the voice of the Lord calling them to discipleship. They themselves were baptized and they were reconciled with their daughter.

When I tell you this, I'm reminded of my Japanese visitor. It was twenty years ago that I met her briefly. And thinking about Lucette Le Goulard and her parents, I think it's quite possible that now, twenty years later in Japan, she may have received the grace of baptism, become an adopted child of God, a sister of ours, and even this day, have taken her place in the Eucharistic assembly. It's possible, because all things are possible with God. And we should pray for that because it is a great good that we should yearn for.

Amen.

14

Falling Asleep at the TV

In the name of the Father, and of the Son,
and of the Holy Spirit.

A millennium is a thousand years, and the year 2000 marked the end of the second millennium and the beginning of the third. One of the things I missed as the 1990s drew to a close was a public acknowledgement of what the second millennium was the second millennium of. The years are numbered, as you probably know, from the birth of Christ, 2000 AD means 2000 Anno Domini. *Anno Domini* is the Latin for "year of our Lord," and the year 2000 marked the end therefore, of two thousand years since the appearing of our Lord, two thousand years of Christian faith and life, and the beginning of a new, third millennium since His appearing.

Unless you are a churchgoing Christian, and even then it depended on which church you were going to, you'd never have known this. I never heard it mentioned publicly; for all the talk about the millennium, its meaning was dismissed.

I do remember movies about the end of the world and terrible things happening. And I remember a television series titled *Millennium*. Sinister forces were out there waiting to erupt when the millennium arrived. Dorothy and I watched that show every week. (That's kind of a public confession. I just want to say right now that I have never watched *The Young and the Restless*, and neither has Dorothy. I just want to say that.)

Of more interest perhaps, was the Great Computer Meltdown. Do you remember that? Somebody told me it was called "Y2K" or something like that, whatever that means. I have no idea what that means. All I know about computers is that I can turn mine on and I can usually turn it off. And the other thing I know about computers is that we can no longer do anything anywhere anymore without them. So when we began to hear rumors that at midnight January 1st, 2000, all the computers of the world might stop functioning, I became concerned. You may remember that we heard reports that the power grid everywhere would cease functioning, cars would stop running—I understand my car has several computers and probably so does yours—planes would fall from the sky, and we wouldn't be able to get our email. (I took that to be the good news.)

Now, ten years later, ten years after the fact, after a

whole decade, it sounds absurd but at the time it was pretty serious, and a lot of smart people who know an awful lot more about these things than I do were talking about this so I was a little alarmed about what was going to happen; it created disquietude.

For me however, the most interesting thing about the coming of the new millennium was thinking about the end of the first millennium. I had read in the history books that the Christians at the end of the first millennium decided it might be the right time for the Lord to return, a thousand years having passed. So they went out and fixed everything up, fixed up the churches, fixed everything up, in order to receive the Lord with joy when He appeared. What a difference a thousand years makes! A thousand years later, Christ was never mentioned and all that was envisioned was catastrophe.

Predicting the future is hazardous business at best, and as for the return of our Lord, He repeatedly said that no one knows when He will appear. In fact, He said He doesn't even know when He will appear. Right? Not the angels, not even the Son of Man, but only the Father knows. (Mt 24:36) Nevertheless, despite our Lord's clarity on this matter, throughout the past two thousand years, there have always been people certain that they knew or know the day and the hour. Right?

My paternal grandfather loved the radio preachers and in childhood I spent a lot of time with him and therefore I also listened to those radio preachers, and while I might have misunderstood them because I was very young, it seemed as though all those radio preachers knew that the coming of the Lord was imminent, and it was not going to be pretty. It took me a long time and a lot of Bible reading to realize that according to our Lord Himself no one knows when He will appear, and that His promise to come again in glory is not supposed to fill us with dread but with joy. In fact the entire Bible ends with this simple prayer which apparently dominated the prayers of the first Christians: "Come, Lord Jesus." (Rev 22:20)

Our reading from the Letter to the Hebrews begins with a famous and much-quoted definition of faith. "Faith is the assurance of things hoped for, the conviction of things not seen." (Heb 11:1) Put another way, to have faith means to believe the Lord God when He makes a promise. That's what Abraham did, and we heard that in the first reading. The Lord made a promise to him and he believed the Lord. And this was accounted to him as righteousness. (Gen 15:6) In that long reading from Hebrews, and I didn't count up all the times the word 'faith' is used, but every time it means to believe God when He makes a promise and to live in the light of that promise.

One of those to whom God made a promise was Sarah the wife of Abraham, and I love this verse embedded in the middle of that long reading.

> By faith, Sarah herself received power to conceive even
> when she was past the age, since she considered Him
> faithful who had promised. (Heb 11:11)

Throughout the Old and New Testaments, the Faithful One is the Lord Himself. He is faithful in that He keeps the promises He makes, in the same way that a faithful husband is one who keeps the promises he made on his wedding day. Our Lord Jesus Christ, the supernatural Bridegroom, has promised us all that He will return in glory to gather us into His Kingdom and to bring history to its conclusion and goal.

Well, we've been waiting for over two thousand years, right? Now, another decade has passed since the millennium was celebrated. And it's easy to give up on the promise, to be persuaded that it's simply not going to happen, that that's one part of our Christian faith that we can kind of not worry about, you know? But of course, to do this means to lose faith in the Faithful One; it means to believe that He will not keep His promise to us, and that we should forget the whole business of His coming again in glory to judge the living and the dead, and to establish His glorious Kingdom—that we should write that off—and instead devote ourselves to other things, and I mean *devote* ourselves to other things, like making heaven-on-earth by our own efforts—and we've seen a lot of that, especially in the last two hundred years—or by surfing,[1] or watching bad television shows. To do this is precisely what our Lord means by "falling asleep" and being asleep at His coming.

To "fall asleep" doesn't mean to literally fall asleep or to become inactive, it means to distract ourselves by doing other things because we have given up on the Lord and His promise. (Mt 25:5) To be awake means to believe that our Lord will keep His promise; to be awake means to remember His promise with joy, to pray for its fulfillment and to live in the light of it.

We cannot believe in Jesus without believing Jesus. We don't know when He will appear and we've been waiting a long time, but to trust Him to keep His promise means to be awake, to be ready when He arrives, and to receive His blessing.

Amen. Come, Lord Jesus.

---

[1] [Transcriber's Footnote:] A particular passion of Fr. Doran, curate at St. Michael's

15

The Secret

*In the name of the Father, and of the Son,
and of the Holy Spirit.*

I have several unwritten books rolling around inside of me. They're there, but they'll never be written because my medium is the spoken word not the written word. And since that's true, I'll tell you about one of those books. The title is, *The Secret Is There Are No Secrets*. By which I mean all that we need to know is known by anyone who cares to look and listen. It's all in what we might call the public domain. And not only is it all known, it's all been known for centuries and millennia.

For example, financial advice is an industry—one by the way that I've profited from a little bit. Books, television, radio programs and seminars abound. For a fee, people will tell us the secret of financial success and well-being. Of course, there really is no secret. The truth is this: we must spend less than we earn. There it is, you heard it here free. That's 98% of everything anybody needs to know to enjoy financial health. All of the seminars and radio programs deal with the other two percent.

Well, truth is indivisible, and what's true for a barista at Starbucks is also true for the rich and famous. Some of you may remember Terry Cole-Whittaker. In the end of the 70's and the beginning of the 80's, she was the queen of the Church of Religious Science here in San Diego County. Well, the Church of Religious Science wasn't actually a church or religious or science, but I live in Vista La Jolla which is not in La Jolla and has no vistas so I'm used to these things.

In any event, I read in the newspaper that she had taken in fifty million dollars. Now that's a lot of money, then or now. But she spent fifty-*five* million, went bankrupt and I haven't heard from her since. See, she knew a lot about money but she had forgotten the fundamental truth that we all need to know and which is there always for everyone.

Fifty years ago, Bernard Goldberg was the principal flutist and bona fide star of the Pittsburgh Symphony. Dorothy, my spouse and a professional flutist was fortunate enough to have studied with him. And I want to tell you a story that was told about him by people who knew him well and who had no reason to make up stories about him. I knew him casually but never asked him if this story was true, but it's credible.

Bernie was a gifted student of the great French flutists who virtually created the modern flute. After finishing his studies in France, he came back to the States and at an early age was hired as principal flutist at the Cleveland Symphony, one of the great orchestras of this nation. Plagued by anxiety, dread, and sleepless nights after beginning his professional career, he went to a psychiatrist seeking relief. The psychiatrist reportedly listened to him and then asked what he did for a living. And when Bernie told him, the psychiatrist said, "What are you doing here? You should be home practicing." He took the doctor's advice and his problems faded.

You know, that story reminds me of an old joke that musicians used to tell when I was young, so it was a long time ago now, about the orchestra that goes to New York and one of the members gets lost, and he's trying to find his way, and he sees a police officer, and he goes up to the policeman and says, "How can I get to Carnegie Hall?" And the policeman looks at his violin case and says, "Practice." See, there are no secrets. That's the secret.

Pio of Pietrelcina, who became known around the world as Padre Pio after his ordination to the priesthood, was a Capuchin friar from southern Italy. (The Capuchins, by the way, have blessed us all with cappuccino. I appreciate it profoundly.) Born in 1887, he died in 1968 and was canonized by John Paul II on June 16, 2002. To say that he was a legend in his own time would be a gross understatement. He was a stigmatist (that is to say, someone who bore in his own flesh the wounds of Christ), and it was widely observed. He received visions from the Lord, fought with the devil, possessed the gift of healing, could read souls, and most interesting of all to me at least, he was known to bilocate (that is to say, to be seen in two different places at the same time), which of course is metaphysically impossible. However, lots of people witnessed this phenomenon.

As you can imagine, people would flock to him from all over the world, people with troubles. I'm sure there were plenty of curiosity seekers, but curiosity seekers usually don't make the effort that people had to make to get to an obscure place in southern Italy to find Padre Pio. So people did go to him from all over the world with their problems and their troubles and their illnesses. And to many of them, a great many of them, so many of them that this became synonymous with his ministry, to many of them he simply said, this visionary, this living saint with the stigmata, "Pray, hope, and don't worry."

That's it! Pray, hope, and don't worry. Can you imagine going halfway around the world to find the great visionary, the stigmatist, and you want to say, "Father, please! I need help! Help me!" And he says, "Pray, hope, and don't worry." You don't need to go around the world to find that out. Right?

This is the pure teaching of our Lord Jesus Christ and the Apostles contained in the gospels and the epistles of the New Testament. And to me, that's the proof that Padre Pio was on the level, that these people came to him and he did not make up some craziness or tell them that he had seen… "Oh, I've seen you in a vision!" No, he told them what he had received from the Lord, and what every one of us can receive from the Lord if we look and listen, if we open our Bibles. Right? Pray, hope, and don't worry.

The secret is, there are no secrets.

The word of the Lord for us today is as simple as the exhortation of Padre Pio or the exhortation of Bernie Goldberg's psychiatrist: put your trust in the Lord and do good. That's it. Do I want to find the peace that the Lord promises me? Do I want to know the joy of the Lord? If so, I need to put my trust in Him and do good. I need to put my trust in Him and do the good that flows from putting my trust in Him.

"Put your trust in the Lord and do good" (Ps 37:3) is a description of our Lord Jesus Christ's life among us in this world, and also a description of His death. During His earthly ministry, our Lord Jesus Christ trusted totally and absolutely in God the Father and went about doing good, both in His life and in His death. "Put your trust in the Lord and do good" is a one sentence description of everything contained in Matthew, Mark, Luke, and John, which they elaborate to give us the particulars.

This is also the word of the Lord given to us this day through the prophet Habakkuk. The reading is a hodgepodge. (Hab 1:1-6,12-13;2:1-4) If you were following it when the reader was reading it, you will notice that they leave out verses. It's a strange hodgepodge because they're trying to get the essentials but it's a little difficult to tell when the Lord is speaking to the prophet, and when the prophet's speaking to the Lord. But this is the story.

Habakkuk lived and prophesied at the height of Babylonian power. (Babylon was also known as Chaldea.) And the prophet seeks to know why the Lord will allow the Babylonians to succeed when they are evil. Here I should point out that in 587 BC the Babylonians invaded Judah, carried off all the leaders, the aristocracy, the priesthood, everyone who was learned into captivity and exile, destroyed the city, and most importantly of all, destroyed the Temple. And this is what causes the prophet to cry out to the Lord, "Why dost Thou look on faithless men and are silent when the wicked swallow up the man more righteous than he?" (Hab 1:13) And the Lord answered him,

Write the vision,

123

> make it plain upon tablets,
>   so he may run who reads it,
> for still the vision awaits its time,
>   it hastens to the end—it will not lie.
> If it seems slow, wait for it.
>   It will surely come, it will not delay.
> Behold, he whose soul is not upright in him
>   shall fail,
>   but the righteous shall live by his faith.
>
> (Hab 2:2-4)

I would paraphrase it this way: The one whose heart is right shall live by trusting in the Lord no matter what the circumstances.

The question that Habakkuk asks about the success of the evil in the world, in the face of the goodness of God, is also addressed by the psalmist at the end of the section of the psalm we read. The psalmist (Ps 37:8-10) tells us,

> Do not fret yourself over the one who prospers,
> the man who succeeds in evil schemes.
> Refrain from anger, leave rage alone.
>   The evildoers will be cut off.

Hear then the word of the Lord. Put your trust in the Lord and do good. And the psalmist elaborates.

Commit your way to the Lord
and put your trust in Him. (Ps 37:5)

Take delight in the Lord. (Ps 37:4)

Be still before the Lord
and wait patiently for Him. (Ps 37:7)

The secret is, there are no secrets.

In today's Gospel, our Lord tells us that a faithful servant does what is commanded of him. (Lk 17:10) And the Lord commands us, his servants, to put our trust in Him absolutely, and to do good. This is the way of peace, joy, goodness, truth, and life. This is this way of Jesus our Lord, Who is the Way, the Truth, and the Life. And should we receive this word as the Lord hopes that we will, and embrace it, our Lord tells us that we should say to the One Who has given us this word of life,

We are unworthy servants; we have only done what was our duty. (Lk 17:10)

Amen.

PART IV

The Identity of God

16

The Hope-Filled God

*In the name of the Father, and of the Son,
and of the Holy Spirit.*

When the First Letter of the apostle Paul to Timothy was
read, we heard these words:

> God our Savior desires all men to be saved and to come
> to the knowledge of the truth. (1Tim 2:3-4)

Believe it or not, this brought to mind a song. (Not one of
those contemporary songs that Fr. Doran knows—I don't
know those songs.) Thirty years ago, I happened to hear this
song. It was an old recording by a jazz trumpet player and
singer named Bunny Berigan. Bunny recorded the song in
1937, and the song was written by Ira Gershwin (George
Gershwin's brother) and Vernon Duke. Ira was the lyricist.
And Bunny Berigan's rendition of this song is still cherished

by jazz fans all through the decades. The title of the song is *I Can't Get Started*. It still makes me smile every time I listen to it. And you can listen to it too on the internet, because everything is on the internet, even Bunny Berigan. (Lots of Bunny Berigan, I discovered.)

Remember, this song was written in 1936, when the celebrity culture was young but already pervasive. These are the lyrics which I will read to you and, mercifully, not sing.

I Can't Get Started

I've flown around the world in a plane,
I've settled revolutions in Spain,
The North Pole I have charted,
But I can't get started with you.

Around the golf course I'm under par,
And all the movies want me to star,
I've got a house that's a showplace,
But I can't get no place with you.[1]

In nineteen twenty-nine I sold short,
In England, I'm presented at court,
Greta Garbo's had me to tea,
I've been consulted by Franklin D.,

---

[1] I just love that part.

Still I'm broken-hearted
'Cause I can't get started with you.

Now you may wonder how in the world the apostle Paul's words concerning God's desire that all should be saved and come to the knowledge of the truth could bring that song to mind, but I ask for your patience.

Aside from the fact that Berigan's rendition really is wonderful, I love the song because it presents us with a dimension of the mystery of love which is seldom discussed or acknowledged explicitly. And it is this: Love always seeks to be requited, but no matter how worthy, how accomplished the one who loves is, it is not always or necessarily reciprocated. Love is a gift, arguably the ultimate gift that anyone can give since it's a gift of the self, but like every gift, it flows from the generosity and the intention of the giver, never from the worthiness of the one to whom it's offered. This is the truth captured by Ira Gershwin in the song *I Can't Get Started*.

The subject has and has done everything desirable and admirable, he is in every way gifted and accomplished, yet these things do not make him lovable to the one to whom his words are addressed. Love resides not in the realm of necessity but in the realm of freedom. One cannot add up one's virtues and demand to be loved. God is love. Those are the words of the apostle St. John found in his first letter (1Jn 4:8,16), and they are a declaration of the mystery of God the Holy Trinity. God is love because He is a tri-personal communion of love. The Father loves the Son eternally in the Spirit, and the Son eternally reciprocates that love to the Father in the same Spirit, and out of this relational love that flows between the Father, Son, and Holy Spirit—a perfect love which makes them One and not three—God created us.

God, Who is always Father since He is never without the Son, wills to extend His Fatherhood, not to add to His own plentitude or fullness, not to add anything to Himself, but for the enrichment of others, namely ourselves. You know, in the Creed we say, "I believe in God, the Father Almighty, creator of heaven and earth," because first, God is Father, He is eternally Father since He always has the Son. But He is not eternally creative, because there was a time when the creation was not, but God was always the Father, Son, and Holy Spirit.

Salvation, Paul tells us, is to share in the divine life, to be taken into the Holy Trinity, to love the Father in and through the Son and with the Son in the Holy Spirit, and to be loved by the Father in the Son through the same Spirit. To be saved, in the distinctly Christian sense of this word, is to live with and in God now and forever as His adopted children. To be saved does not mean to receive something from God, but to receive God Himself, to receive a place in God, and to share in His eternal life.

This is what the Christian sacraments are all intended to impart. When we receive Holy Communion, we do not receive something, we receive Someone. God is everything good and the source of all good but, as in the song *I Can't Get Started*, this does not necessarily mean that we will reciprocate His love, that we will return it, or want to share in His life now or forever. And so St. Paul tells us that God desires all men to be saved and come to the knowledge of the truth. But this does not mean that all men will be saved and come to the knowledge of the truth.

It doesn't sound right, but it is apparently true that God hopes that we will respond to and reciprocate His love. Hope, like faith and love, is a truth about God Himself.

Charles Péguy was a French poet of the early 20th century, and he expressed this particular mystery of God in a poem titled *The Portal of the Mystery of Hope*. Aidan Nichols, a scholar and theologian, has observed that,

> making hope an attribute of God is a thoroughly audacious move, yet the witness of revelation is that God, Who in no ordinary sense can need anything at all—not even the entirety of His creation—does, in some extraordinary sense, long for us, such that this love-longing of God for us is the primary presupposition of the whole story of salvation.

David Schindler, another great scholar, also commenting on this wrote,

> According to Péguy, God too is joined with His creation in hoping. He has entered into creation out of love, and asks His creatures to respond in love, and this means in freedom; since freedom is essential to love, God cannot force Himself on the one He loves. Instead, He Himself is forced to await the freedom of His creature, forced to hope for the sinner.

This is, in fact, of course the point of the Parable of the Prodigal Son which is so familiar to all of us. The loving father cannot impose himself on the son; the son rejects the father and leaves, and the father waits in hope for the son to return. No one can give what he does not possess, not even God. St. Paul tells us that the higher gifts of the Holy Spirit are faith, hope, and love; and in order to give these gifts God Himself must possess them.

God desires all men to be saved and come to the knowledge of the truth. Salvation and the truth are inseparable, for Jesus the Savior is Himself the Way, the Truth, and the Life. God desires all men to be saved and come to the knowledge of the truth. The truth is, St. Paul goes on to tell us, that there is one God, and there is one mediator between God and men, the man Christ Jesus, Who gave Himself on the cross as a ransom for all.

Again, I want you to notice that the Lord did not offer Himself to the Father on the cross for some of us, but for all of us, meaning all people from the first to the last.

Through the centuries the Church has rejected Universalism, the belief that everyone in the end will be saved. This idea which has no foundation anywhere in holy scripture, is based on a notion that since God is love, then He couldn't damn anyone; it just wouldn't be nice.

The words of St. Paul in the First Letter to Timothy are a sobering reminder that God rejects no one but that we can reject God, and so become separated from Him in time and eternity, which is the whole meaning of damnation. The drama of God and man found in scripture and experienced in life is that God loves His creature Man and wants to live in union with Him while Man prefers himself to God.

The story would be sad and tragic if God were passive, but the God Who made us is always present and active, He is always seeking us, always hoping that we will turn to Him as He is always turned to us, so that we can be saved and come to the knowledge of the truth. The possibility of eternal separation from God is real, but let us hope and pray with the true and living God, the Father, Son, and Holy Spirit, that everyone will be saved and come to the knowledge of the truth.

Amen.

17

Forgiveness Takes Two

In the name of the Father, and of the Son,
and of the Holy Spirit.

Do you remember the saying, "It takes two to tango?" I don't hear that as much as I used to, but you may remember it. It does take two to tango, and like the tango, forgiveness takes two. Forgiveness is a relational act, and it involves at least two people.

Twenty years ago or so, I had a mother come to me in great distress. She had a daughter who was an affliction in her life and in everyone else's life. From an early age, the daughter had been involved with drugs... criminals... often brought home by the police... refused to do anything in school... The list goes on and on, and the mother had dealt with this for a very long time, and finally came to me greatly disturbed. I assumed it was about the behavior of her daughter, because I was well acquainted with the situation. But it turned out that it was not only the behavior of her daughter that was disturbing to her. She came to me in some distress because, as she said, "I have always forgiven my daughter. I have always forgiven her, just as I have always been taught to do as a member of the church, and it has done no good whatsoever. In fact, she goes from bad to worse."

It's true that forgiveness is at the heart of Christianity. We are often exhorted to forgive—sometimes to forgive and to forget. Our Lord told Peter that he is to forgive his brother not seven times but seven times seventy. (A Swedish movie producer made a movie, I think it was in the early Sixties, with the title *491*. I'll leave it to you to meditate on that!) The Lord teaches us to pray, "Forgive us our sins as we forgive those who sin against us." And our Lord, of course, died on the cross in order to win for us forgiveness.

And so it is that this mother highly distraught said: all of this is so and I have believed all of this and I have always forgiven my daughter. To what end?

After I talked to her for some time, I finally asked her, "Has your daughter ever said she was sorry? Has she ever acknowledged the terrible things she has done? Has she ever sought to change? Has she ever asked you to forgive her?" In other words, had she ever repented of any of the things she had done? And the answer was, no. The daughter, if anything, was arrogant about her behavior, and certainly had not asked for forgiveness.

So the mother had never actually forgiven her daughter—not because she had not tried, not because she did not desire to forgive her, not because she was unwilling to forgive, but because *the daughter could not receive the forgiveness*. Forgiveness is not a unilateral act; it is a relational act between the offender and the offended, between the sinner and the one who has been sinned against. And the goal of forgiveness is reconciliation, the healing of the relationship. Listen to this word from our Lord that is particularly important, because it is clarifying.

> If your brother sins against you (says the Lord), go and tell him his fault, between you and him alone. If he listens to you (IF HE LISTENS TO YOU!) you have gained your brother. (Mt 18:15)

"If he listens to you" means, if he acknowledges his transgression and seeks your forgiveness. And now we have the repentant offender and the forgiving offended, and we have won our brother. The two can be reconciled.

Forgiveness is not an end in itself, it is a means to an end. The end is reconciliation with the one who has sinned. Sin always destroys relationships, both with God and with our neighbor, and forgiveness has as its goal the healing of that wound.

However, our Lord makes it clear that the transgressor is always free to say, "No, I do not want to be forgiven, I have done nothing that requires forgiveness." And the Lord says in this teaching about relationships between Christians in the Church that first, we should talk to the person in private with the hope that the person will listen. Then we should take witnesses and finally we should go to the Church and if the person still says "no, I will not listen," then "let him be to you as a Gentile and a tax collector," that is, one with whom you have no relationship, because that person has turned away and has broken the bond that has existed. (cf. Mt 18:15-17)

You know, this is not all that mysterious. All of us who have had children may have had this experience. I'll use the example of the mother and the child. (That's only because I don't bake.) The mother bakes cookies. She puts them on the kitchen counter to cool and she says to the child, "Don't eat a cookie. It'll spoil your appetite." (Have you ever noticed how mothers are preoccupied with our appetites? You know, my father never said, "You'll spoil your appetite!" Well, that's something to think about at another time.) In any event, the mother says, "You'll spoil your appetite! You can have a cookie for dessert after dinner." She goes about her business. A while later she returns. There's a cookie missing of course, and she says to the child, "Didn't I tell you not to eat a cookie?" And the child says, "I didn't!"

And then it starts, right?

"Well, clearly, there are only two of us here. One of us ate the cookie, and it wasn't me," says the mother.

The child says, "Well, it wasn't me."

Now, parents usually fall back to the next line, which is: "It's worse to lie to me, than to have eaten a cookie." Right? How many of us have said this! "Just admit you ate the cookie. Don't lie—that's even worse than eating the cookie. I'm not going to lock you in the attic or throw you into the basement. There's no dire consequence here. Just admit you ate it and then I can say, 'It's okay. Don't do it again.' And we can go on."

But no, the child says, "No, I didn't do it." (Perhaps it was the dog. The dog ate it. The same dog who will several years later eat the homework.)

Now the mother and the child are at an impasse. There is a rift, and there's really nothing a parent can do. As long as the child says 'no,' the mother really cannot forgive the child. And this is also true of God and His relationship with us.

God Himself cannot forgive the impenitent sinner, and that's a fact. Because to be impenitent means to turn away from God—to turn our back on God—and say, "I don't want it. I don't need it. I'm okay." The Lord God expresses this clearly through the prophet Ezekiel. He said,

> I have no pleasure in the death of the wicked, but that
> the wicked turn from his way and live. (Ezek 33:11)

That's exactly what repentance is. The Lord is saying, 'I do not wish the death of the sinner but that he should turn... turn from his evil... turn to me... and live.' But until the wicked man turns from his wickedness to the Lord, the Lord cannot forgive him, not because the Lord does not will his good or desire to forgive him but because the man will not accept that forgiveness, will not receive it. Therefore, we seek the Lord's forgiveness praying (in the prayerbook), "We acknowledge and bewail our manifold sins and wickedness which we from time to time most grievously have committed by thought, word, and deed." Or alternately, and more simply, "Most merciful God, we confess that we have sinned against Thee in thought, word, and deed." And the formula of absolution reads, "Almighty God, our heavenly Father, Who of His great majesty hath promised forgiveness of sins to all those who with hearty repentance and true faith turn unto Him, have mercy upon you."

In order to receive the forgiveness of God, we must turn to Him, acknowledging our transgressions, the goal being to restore us to the grace of baptism, when we became adopted sons and daughters of God, and inheritors of eternal life.

Now there are certain things that flow from this understanding. The first one is this, and it's a difficult one, and easily misunderstood: We cannot forgive the dead. Neither can the dead forgive us.

If someone has wounded us terribly and is unrepentant, and then dies in that impenitence, we cannot forgive them because they are not here to receive it. It would mean that forgiveness is a unilateral act, something that I could do apart from the other who has transgressed. Likewise, if I have transgressed against someone, and I am impenitent and they die, they cannot forgive me, because they are not here to do it.

Now, for all of us who have been terribly wounded by someone who has been impenitent and died, there can be healing. We can be healed, but the proper term for that healing is something other than 'forgiveness.' A couple of weeks ago, the local paper published an article called, "The Healing Power of Forgiveness," but unfortunately, the healing they were talking about did not come from forgiveness. It was really about that healing that takes place in us when we are able to let go of anger and resentment and all the other things that well up in us when somebody has wronged us terribly.

Secondly, we cannot forgive groups. There is no such thing as collective guilt. You know, in the early 1930's, 1932–

142

1933, Stalin and his gang of criminals, who had named the bourgeois class as a group guilty of all sin, set out to destroy the Ukrainian middle class, called the kulaks. And in this winter of 1932–33, Stalin and his people killed seven million Ukrainians in an attempt to destroy this group which had been stigmatized as guilty.

A few years later of course, the Führer said that the Jews and the Gypsies were collectively guilty of all sin and tried to destroy all of them, killing millions more people.

After the war, there have been people who wanted to say that the German nation was collectively guilty. There are people that want to say that the white race is collectively guilty. There are people who are always looking for collectives to hold guilty but collectives are not guilty. Members of those collectives certainly may be guilty, but the collectives themselves are not, because sin is always intensely personal. I sin, and you sin. And it is a personal act. And it is sinning against someone or some people.

Because of this, we cannot repent of what others do, or have done. We cannot repent of what our ancestors have done, or those who come after us. I cannot repent of the sins of my father, or my grandfather, or my son. Those sins are theirs, and they must be borne by them. (Could you imagine if I were to pray, "I confess, O Lord, that Father Moquin has sinned in thought, word, and deed?" What would that be?)

I cannot repent of the sins of another. I can recognize them. I could identify them. I may denounce them. But I cannot repent of them. The goal of repentance is always the healing of relationship, and therefore I can only repent of those things which I have done, in the hope that the one I have transgressed against will forgive me, and that the relationship can be healed.

We cannot forgive people for sins they have not committed. And we cannot repent of sins which we have not committed. The goal of forgiveness is reconciliation. And the only person who can receive the gift of forgiveness is the one who has repented and therefore, is able to receive that gift so that the relationship might be healed and restored.

If we sin against God and our neighbor (and to sin against God is always to sin against our neighbor), we must acknowledge that sin. It is imperative that we do, and turn from this sin to the one that we have wronged, seeking reconciliation.

If we have been sinned against, we have an obligation, the Lord tells us, to go to the one who has sinned against us in the hopes that that person will listen to us and repent, so that we can forgive and so that the relationship may be healed. And I believe that the Lord asks us to do that because that's exactly what the Lord does for each of us. Forgiveness takes two.

Amen.

18

Corpus Christi

In the name of the Father, the Son, and the Holy Spirit.

I received from the Lord what I also delivered to you, that the Lord Jesus on the night when He was betrayed took bread and, when He had given thanks, He broke it and said, "This is My body which is for you."

1Cor 11:23-24

Corpus Christi is Latin for the body of Christ, and the importance of the body of Christ and of our bodies cannot really be overstated. We do not have bodies, we are bodies; we are embodied souls. That's how St. Thomas Aquinas described human beings, as embodied—or incarnate—souls. Angels (like ghosts) on the other hand, are disembodied—or disincarnate—spirits. And therefore what happens to our bodies, happens to us. Socrates, a Greek, a pagan, and one of my favorite people, was not an Israelite, and so he supposed that the body was a prison of the soul, and that death would finally release the soul from its imprisonment in the body. In the great religions of the East, the body is understood to be something that's perpetually replaced like a worn out suit of clothes, that's exactly how the great teachers of Hinduism and Buddhism speak of the body, like a suit of clothes that we wear out and get rid of and then get a new one, over and over again. This is known as reincarnation.

When our Lord rose bodily from the dead, God revealed that the body is neither a prison of the soul nor a suit of clothes that we wear out and get rid of in order to get a new suit. Our Lord Jesus Christ is not only an incarnate and embodied soul like all human beings, He is the eternal word of God made flesh; He is God the Son and having become embodied, He offered His body to God the Father for us and our salvation. His offering was accepted in what we know as the Resurrection and Ascension of His body. In the person of Jesus the Son of God and the son of Mary, God is eternally embodied; Jesus is forever true God and true man.

We say in the Creed that we believe in the resurrection of the body, not only our Lord's body but our own. And out of this faith has come all manner of things that we all take for granted, among them, hospitals and western medical care which has now spread throughout the world. Hospitals and the great concern of our western civilization for the health and welfare of the body, flow from the bodily resurrection of our Lord and, by extension, from the Holy Eucharist. Hospitals are a creation of Christian faith and civilization.

Today in our post-Christian and materialist civilization, if we can call it that, we have now an obsession with the body, with its health and its appearance, that flows not from faith but from a denial of the existence of the soul and a conviction that the body is all there is. You know, for decades now, as I've been driving to church on Sunday morning, I see those body-addicts (as I call them) out there running, and I always want to stop them and say, "If you're not on your way to church, you're running straight to the grave." I haven't done it yet! They might become outraged by that. Anyway, it's the truth, though. If we are just soulless bodies, out there trying to preserve our health and our appearance as long as possible, it's all really pointless.

Our bodies, yours and mine, are forever. They are the means of human presence, identity, and relationship with both God and man and, as such, have been created by God for both time and eternity for this world and for the next. When our Lord returns in glory to judge the living and the dead and to establish His kingdom, He will return as an embodied spirit just as He was when He appeared to His disciples in the Resurrection and departed from them in the Ascension. And on the last day, we will appear before Him as embodied souls just as we do today.

In order to be present for you, I have to get my body into some kind of proximity to yours. If I tell you, "I'll be with you in spirit," I'm telling you that my body will be somewhere else and so will all the rest of me. Or to put it another way, if I tell you that I'll be with you in spirit, I'm telling you *I won't be with you.*

If I want to find you, I must find your body, because there is no 'you' apart from it. And as this is so for our relationship with one another, it's true for our relationship with our Lord Jesus Christ. If we want to find Him and be found by Him, know Him, be with Him, and be related to Him, we need to find His body for there is no Jesus apart from His body any more than there is a 'you' apart from your body. And all this brings us to the Feast of Corpus Christi, the feast of the body of Christ, and to the Mass.

The Mass, or Holy Eucharist, is the sacrament of the bodily presence of our Lord. He has given it to us so that He Himself can be found, so that we can find Him, be with Him, receive Him, and share in His eternal life with God the Father and the Holy Spirit.

Our Lord is present for us in the Eucharist in order that His body can become one body with our bodies, so that we can become the body of Christ. He wants to share Himself, all of Himself, with us in order that we can share all of ourselves with Him and live with Him now and forever. Without His bodily presence manifested in the Eucharist, we could not find Him, be with Him, share our lives with Him, or share in His life now or forever. Without the Eucharist, He would be with us in spirit, which is to say, *He would not be with us at all.*

> Truly, truly, I say to you, he who believes has eternal life. I am the bread of life. Your fathers ate manna in the wilderness and they died. This is the bread which comes down from heaven that a man may eat of it and not die. I am the living bread which came down from heaven. If anyone eats of this bread, he will live forever and the bread which I shall give for the life of the world is my flesh. (Jn 6:47-51)

Amen.

19

Who Is Jesus?

In the name of the Father, and of the Son,
and of the Holy Ghost.

I suspect that we have all had encounters in our lives that have changed us. When I was sixteen years old, I had a really life-changing encounter for which I'm profoundly grateful. I was killing time before going to an after-school job, and I was doing it at a bookstore (a habit that I have never broken). In any event, I went in there and, browsing among the books, picked up a copy of *Crime and Punishment*, one of the great novels of the Russian author Fyodor Dostoevsky. And over the next four or five years, I read all of his major works and many of his minor works and have been profoundly influenced by him, permanently changed by that encounter with someone in literature.

I've looked back on it and thought it could have been simply a coincidence. Maybe I was attracted by the lurid

WHO IS JESUS?

cover on the 95¢ paperback. (Boy those were the good old days.) But I really don't believe in such coincidences; I think it was providential, really.

And in the many many pages of Dostoevsky somewhere, I encountered a passage where he says, "The one life and death question, the one life and death question which everyone must ultimately answer: Who is Jesus?" Not, "What did Jesus do?" but "Who is Jesus?"

I remember years ago, maybe twenty years ago, *Time Magazine* published an issue with a portrait of our Lord on the cover and under his portrait it had the question, "Who was Jesus?" That's an entirely different question, right? And it prejudices the answer, and in fact, the question 'who was Jesus?' already tells us the answer. He's someone who is dead. Right? He's someone from the past, like Socrates or Napoleon. But the real question, the question we all have to answer is, "Who is He?"

Today, John the Baptist identifies Him, identifies Him in three complementary ways. First, he begins by identifying Jesus as the Lamb of God, the Lamb of God Who takes away the sins of the world. (Jn 1:29) Secondly, he identifies Him as the Son of God. (Jn 1:34) And finally, as the Messiah. And by the way, St. John likes to tell us what the Hebrew words mean by translating them into Greek words, so he says He is the Messiah, which means the Christ. (Jn 1:41) Of course, what he's telling the Greeks is that Messiah is the Hebrew for Anointed One, which is what *Christos* means.

151

So for us who are not Greek speakers, the Messiah means the Anointed One of God, the One Who has been anointed by the Holy Spirit.

℀

First, we are. And then, we do. The seasons of Christmas and Epiphany are an annual meditation on the identity of our Lord Jesus Christ. In the seasons of Lent, by the way, and Holy Week, we meditate on what He did. But what He did doesn't make much sense unless we know Who He is. The important question is, "Who is He?" And so John identifies Him for us, repetitiously and in complementary ways.

The world is full of people, and always has been ever since our Lord appeared, who have opinions about Him and about what He did. Hence the *Time Magazine* article where all these people give their opinions about who Jesus was. And when they talk about who He was, of course, they're talking about what He did and what they think of it, but our Lord's deeds are inseparable from His identity. It's from His identity, His being as the Son of God, the Messiah, and the Lamb of God, that His deeds emerge. And unless we know who He is, we will not understand what He did. His deeds are inseparable from His identity.

And so from the moment of His birth, the cross is present because our Lord came into the world, was sent by the Father, to bear the cross. Already at Christmas (which exists, and the Christmas stories in the Gospels exist, to proclaim the identity of Jesus) the cross is announced. Our Lord is born under the shadow of the cross, because the Father sent Him into the world to bear the cross. Therefore at His birth, there is no room for Him at the inn, as we know. And He's born on the very edge of the human race, in a stable with animals, already a sign that there will be no room for Him in the world, and that at the end finally, thirty-three years later, the world will cast Him out of the city and crucify Him.

And then there's the story of the Magi who come bearing their wonderful gifts of gold, frankincense, and myrrh, and they're warned in a dream by an angel to flee from Herod who is about to kill the child Jesus. St. John the Baptist, before he proclaims Jesus as the Son of God and the Messiah, announces Him to be the Lamb of God. And who is the Lamb of God who takes away the sins of the world? Our Lord, Who will offer Himself for the life of the world on the cross, in an act of perfect obedience and love for God the Father.

Our Lord's deeds are inseparable from His identity. Our Lord is anointed by the Holy Spirit; He is the Messiah, the Christ, the Anointed One. He is anointed by the Holy Spirit to take up His cross and to do what the human race always fails to do, which is trust God the Father even unto death, believing as He does, that the Father will raise Him from the dead on the third day.

This is what the Letter to the Hebrews means when it tells us that Jesus is like us in every way without sinning.

(Heb 4:15) "He is like us in every way without sinning" means that His deeds, His behavior, His actions, flow always from His identity as the Son of God with perfect coherence. In other words, He never contradicts His identity by His words or His deeds. All of His words and deeds are an expression of His identity as the Lamb of God, the Son of God, and the Anointed One of God.

Those of us who recognize the face of God in the face of Jesus and who know Who He is are in turn identified by Him and are called to be like Him. In today's Gospel, Simon Bar-Jona, Simon the son of John, whose Hebrew name is given, is identified by our Lord, given a new identity. Our Lord says, "From now on you will be called *Cephas*," Hebrew for *Petros*, which in Greek means 'the Rock.' "Peter" means "the Rock." Jesus identifies him: "From now on you shall be Peter, the Rock, on which I will build My Church." (Mt 16:18)

And so as we identify the Lord, the Lord identifies us and gives us an identity, a supernatural identity. In Second Corinthians, the apostle Paul wrote, "Though He was rich, yet for our sake He became poor so that by His poverty we might become rich." (2Cor 8:9) And the Church Fathers commented on this over and over and over again. He became as we are so that we might become as He is. He became the son of Mary so that we might become sons and daughters of God. When we were baptized, we were sacramentally united with the Lamb of God in His act of self-offering to the Father in love on the cross, and therefore made His brothers and sisters, adopted children of God, which is exactly what the Catechism tells us. It's the first thing it says about Holy Baptism, that it's the sacrament by which we become adopted children of God.

Therefore we receive a supernatural identity; we are brothers and sisters of the Son of God, temples of the Holy Spirit, children of God the Father.

> See what love the Father has given us, that we should be called children of God, (writes St. John) and so we are. (1Jn 3:1)

And when he says "we," that "we should be called children of God," he means those who have received the grace of baptism and been adopted by God the Father and made brothers and sisters of God the Son, and temples of the Holy Spirit.

St. Paul tells us that the Holy Spirit we received at baptism is the spirit of adoption given to us so that our spirits can cry out with the Holy Spirit, "Abba, Father." (Gal 4:6) And our Lord Jesus Christ says, "When you pray say, 'Father.'" (Lk 11:2) And to say "Father" means to be a child of the One that we name "Father."

To be baptized is to be adopted by God the Father of our Lord Jesus Christ and therefore baptism, which we call a sacrament, is in fact a life to be lived, the life in Christ. To sin means precisely to behave in a manner that contradicts who we are. To confess our sins and be absolved means to be restored to our baptismal identities as children of God, to be restored to our true and eternal identity. To live our baptism means to daily strive with our Lord's help to reconcile our thoughts, words, and deeds with our supernatural identity as the children of God, to become the people God created us and adopted us to be. And this is a lifelong process which will only be completed when we see God face to face in the land of the just, in the Kingdom of the blessed.

To paraphrase St. Augustine: our Lord and God, the Father, Son, and Holy Spirit, has called each of us to become who we are, His children by grace.

Let us pray.

> Almighty and ever-living Father, grant that we, having been born again by water and the Spirit, and made your children by adoption and grace, may daily be renewed by Your Holy Spirit. We ask this through our beloved brother and Lord Jesus Christ, Who lives and reigns with You in the unity of the Holy Spirit, one God, now and unto unending ages of ages.

Amen.

20

Listen

In the name of the living God: the Father,
the Son, and the Holy Spirit.

After six days, (after Peter had acknowledged Jesus as
the Christ, the Son of the living God,) Jesus took with
Him Peter and James and John, his brother, and led
them up a high mountain apart; and He was transfig-
ured before them, and His face shone like the sun, and
his garments became white as light.

Mt 17:1-2

Mountains have always been and remain places of mystery,
places of revelation, and of nearness to the divine. The pagan Greeks of course worshipped their pantheon on Mt.
Olympus, and the new pagans today gather around Mt.
Shasta, which they believe to be a sacred place. And if you
go to Mt. Shasta at the right time, it's easy to see why.

Mountains abound in holy scripture. There is, of course, in the Old Testament, first and foremost, Mt. Sinai. We heard, in the first reading (Ex 24:12-18), of Moses being beckoned by God to ascend the mountain into the cloud of the divine presence, there to enter into intimacy with the Lord God, and to receive from Him instruction, the word of the Lord, which he was to bear to Israel, the people waiting at the foot of the mountain. Then there is Mt. Moriah where the Lord God commanded Abraham to sacrifice his only son Isaac. And Mt. Carmel where Elijah entered into controversy with the priests of Baal, and where God supported him by a miracle.

Mountains abound in the New Testament, and in the life of our Lord, although they're somewhat easy to miss. There is the Mount of Temptation where the devil took our Lord up to a high mountain to show Him all the kingdoms of the world. There is of course the mountain of His great sermon which takes its name from that place, the Sermon on the Mount, which we have been listening to for the last several weeks. There is the mountain of our Lord's prayer where He ascends to enter into intimacy with God the Father. There is of course then the Mount of the Transfiguration which we are remembering this day. And there is the Mount of Olives which is the mountain of His agony. And there is the mountain of His passion and death, Mt. Calvary. And finally the mountain of the resurrection and ascension of our Lord where He declares, "All power in heaven and earth has been given to Me." (Mt 28:18) ℓ

But in order to grasp the meaning of the Transfiguration, we have to go back down the mountain; we have to go back in time. All the evangelists link the Transfiguration with Peter's confession that Jesus is the Christ and the Son of the living God. It is only after Peter and the others can identify Jesus in this way that He begins to teach them what His messiahship is about. He begins to teach them that He has to go to Jerusalem, fall into the hands of evil men, be crucified, die, and raised on the third day. Matthew, Mark, and Luke all link the Transfiguration to this event. And after teaching His disciples the nature of His mission, the reason why He came into the world—to bear the cross—He declared to them, "Truly I say to you, there are some standing here who will not taste death before they see the Son of Man coming in His Kingdom." (Mt 16:28) And six days after Peter had acknowledged Jesus as the Christ and the Son of the living God, He took Peter, James, and John up on the mountain of the Transfiguration.

It is on the Mount of the Transfiguration that Peter, James, and John see Jesus the Messiah and Son of God in His glory; they see the Kingdom in all its power. And it's no wonder therefore that Peter declares, "Lord, it is well that we are here." (Mt 17:4) And he wants to stay because he has seen that which God has promised to those who love Him.

As Moses ascended Mt. Sinai and entered into the cloud of the divine presence known as the shekinah and there received God's instructions, so Peter, James, and John behold Jesus—God's instruction made flesh, the Word of God made man, God's instruction for the new Israel—in glory.

It's most significant of course that Jesus appears with Moses and Elijah, the symbols, the embodiment, of the Law and the Prophets of the old covenant. After His resurrection, He would say that everything written about Him in the Law and the Prophets had to be fulfilled.

And then there is the heavenly voice, the voice of the Father, "This is My beloved Son with Whom I am well pleased." Those are the words that the Father spoke at the baptism of our Lord, exactly the same words; and so in the Transfiguration coming from the cloud of the presence that surrounds our Lord in glory, they hear the voice of the Father, "This is My beloved Son with Whom I am well pleased." (Mt 17:5) But after this proclamation of the identity of Jesus, the Father adds a command at the Transfiguration, "Listen to Him." I believe that this is the word of God for us here and now, for you and for me. God the Father is telling us, as He told Peter, James, and John two thousand years ago on the Mount of the Transfiguration, Who His Son is, and that we should listen to Him.

To listen means to listen attentively, receptively and, when necessary, obediently. When my own father complained that I didn't listen to him, he didn't mean that I was having trouble with my aural faculties. Right? I can still hear him saying that, you know. "You don't listen!" It means that I didn't pay attention, and I didn't do the things he told me to do or abstain from the things that he told me to abstain from, and that's exactly the force of God the Father's words when He tells us to listen to His beloved Son with Whom He is well pleased.

To listen to our Lord as the Father commands us to do is not easy. Two weeks ago I mentioned[1] that I have trouble listening to Him when He says,

> Do not resist one who is evil. (Mt 5:39)

After making that confession, I was somewhat afraid that I might have scandalized those of you who heard me say that and I pray that I didn't; it wasn't my intention. Those of us who love peace and want to see peace in the world may find it very hard to listen when our Lord says,

> Do not think that I have come to bring peace on earth;
> I have not come to bring peace but a sword. (Mt 10:34)

Or what about all of us who love our families and find meaning in life through the relationships with those nearest

---

[1] [Transcriber's Footnote:] See *The Hardest Word*, p. 169

and dearest to us? We certainly might have trouble listening to these words of our Lord:

> I have come to set a man against his father, and daughter against her mother, and a daughter-in-law against her mother-in-law; he who loves father or mother more than Me is not worthy of Me, and he who loves son or daughter more than Me is not worthy of Me. (Mt 10:37)

If you find it easy to listen to that, see me after mass; I want to talk to you.

If at times we find it difficult to listen to the Lord, we need to know that we're in good company. I've already mentioned that the Transfiguration follows Peter's confession that Jesus is the Messiah and the Son of the living God. When Jesus told Peter and the others that being Messiah and the Son of God meant that He had to go to Jerusalem, be rejected, killed, and raised from the dead, Peter immediately rejected every word the Lord said and began to argue with Him. It says, "He rebuked Him." And our Lord said, "Get behind me, Satan; you're not on the side of God but on the side of men." Or to put it another way, Peter refused to listen; he would not receive that word from the Lord. And Peter and the apostles repeatedly were deaf to our Lord when He told them that He had to go to Jerusalem, be rejected, crucified, and raised on the third day. (cf. Mt 16:21-23)

162

When our Lord told His disciples that unless they ate His flesh and drank His blood they would have no life in Him, they said to one another,

This is a hard saying, who can listen to it?

Who can listen to it? Afterwards, St. John tells us, many of the Lord's disciples drew back and no longer went about with Him. (Jn 6:66) Not surprisingly, at one point in His public ministry, our Lord said,

Why do you call me 'Lord, Lord' and not do what I tell you? (Lk 6:46)

Jesus the eternal Son of God listens always to His heavenly Father and He said, "I came not to do My Own will, but the will of Him Who sent Me." (Jn 6:38) On the mountain of His agony, the Mount of Olives, where He took Peter, James, and John—the same three that He took up on the mountain of the Transfiguration—our Lord prayed, "Father, let this cup pass from Me, but not My will, Your will be done." (Mt 26:39) Jesus' entire life among us was one of attentive, receptive, and obedient listening, and the One to Whom He listened calls us to listen to Him. "This is My beloved Son with Whom I am well pleased; listen to Him." (Mt 17:5)

The disciples and apostles of our Lord spent their entire lives learning to listen to the Lord, and it took them time and it shouldn't surprise us if it takes us time. I think it takes a lifetime (a sure sign of our fallen condition, that it takes us all our lives) to learn to listen attentively, receptively, and finally obediently, to our Lord Jesus Christ.

This Wednesday is Ash Wednesday. We are at the end of the Epiphany season and stand near the beginning of Lent, and Lent is the season when we're all called back to the basics, a kind of spring training for Christians. We're exhorted to return to the basic disciplines of our faith: prayer, fasting, and good works. But all of these are meant to help us listen more attentively to our Lord. They're not ends in themselves, they are a means. When our Lord was asked, "What must we do to be doing the works of God?" He replied, "This is the work of God, that you believe in the One Whom He has sent." (Jn 6:28-29) And to believe in the One Whom He has sent is inseparable from that attentive, receptive, obedient listening which the Father commands.

St. Basil the Church Father, says that there are three dispositions with which one can obey (that is, listen). The first is fear of punishment, as in the case of slaves. The second is a desire for reward, as in the case of mercenaries. The third one is out of love and this is the attitude of sons and daughters. This third disposition, as St. Basil calls it, is the disposition of Jesus, the Son Who loves His Father and Who was obedient to Him, even unto death, death on a cross.

164

Diadochos of Photike, a desert father, (and by the way, is that not a mouthful?) observed that, "It is through obedience that we are not only in the image of God but like to God."

> This is My beloved Son with Whom I am well pleased, (says the Father). Listen to Him. (Mt 17:5)

May the Holy Spirit purify our hearts and our minds and give us ears to hear.

Amen.

Appendix

TRANSCRIBER'S NOTE: *This sermon is unlike the others, not that its message is any different (actually, it's quite an appropriate summation of this collection, touching as it does many themes already encountered: close reading of Scripture, trust, God's identity and the Christian's) but the reader may notice a concise style due to this being the original prepared text[1] and not a transcript of its delivery at a service. As this was not recorded, no transcription will ever be available. "Alexander S." would be Alexander Solzhenitsyn—one doesn't need to spell out what isn't for printing. ;-) So, here is a "backstage" example, the written stage, the unimprovised portion, the bare-bones skeleton, of the sermon Fr. Kraft gave on the Seventh Sunday after the Epiphany 2011 (February 20).*

---

[1] The author's own title as found on his printout:
"YOU MUST BE PERFECT AS YOUR HEAVENLY FATHER IS PERFECT."

21

The Hardest Word

David Adams Richards' *The Lost Highway* contains this remarkable piece of dialogue.

> Once when Burton was frightened because he had
> heard there was going to be a war, and actually started
> crying though he didn't want to, Mrs. Chapman had
> smiled and said; "Dear Burton—don't you know we
> have always been at war?"
>
> "Where?" Burton had asked.
>
> Mrs. Chapman pointed at her heart.

Alexander S. who suffered for years as a slave laborer in the
concentration camps of the Soviet Union observed that the
line between good and evil runs through the human heart
and it is in the heart that the unseen warfare, as Mrs. Chap-

man indicates, and the Word of God constantly reminds us, takes place.

Today's Gospel is a continuation of our reading of the Sermon on the Mount, a continuation of the antitheses we began reading last Sunday in which our Lord, the Messiah and Son of God, declares his Torah or Law. Moses was the bearer of the Torah or God's instructions received on Mount Sinai. Now Jesus announces His own Torah, renewing and intensifying the Law in a series of declarations, "You have heard that is was said, ...But I say to you...".

Only God, who is the giver of the Law, could claim to be its definitive interpreter. And the interpretive key to the Sermon on the Mount is our Lord's declaration that he did not come to abolish the Law and the Prophets but to fulfill them in his own person.

> You have heard that it was said, 'You shall love your
> neighbor and hate your enemy.' But I say to you, Love
> your enemies and pray for those who persecute you.

"You shall love your neighbor" is a commandment found in the book of Leviticus Ch.19, verse 18. "You shall hate your enemy" is not found in the Law of Moses. Here our Lord is referring to the widespread rabbinical interpretation of Lev. 19:18 which understood "neighbor" to refer only to fellow

Israelites. (This interpretation was explicitly rejected by our Lord in the Parable of the Good Samaritan.) "But I say to you, Love your enemies and pray for those who persecute you."

Now this is the easy part of today's Gospel. Easy, that is, if we understand first of all, that our Lord is not asking us to like our enemies. God does not call us to like anyone. THANK YOU LORD. (Here I should point out that it's possible to love people without liking them—being a member of a family is to be enrolled in a school that teaches this truth). On the other hand we can like people without loving them. When our Lord refers to love he is most emphatically not referring to a state of the emotions. To love means to desire and seek the good of the other. This love, to steal a line from Marriage Encounter, is not a state of the emotions but an act of the will. To put it in plain language, if I see a man robbing another at gun point, I do not love the criminal by ignoring, minimizing or excusing his behavior, but by calling the police and praying he's arrested and punished. This is the "good" which I am called by love to desire and will for him. It is also the way I love his victim. So, no, we are not being asked by our Lord to cultivate warm feelings of affection for our enemies and those who persecute us, or to excuse or ignore their bad behavior.

For me the real difficulty is found these words spoken by our Lord.

> You have heard that it was said, 'An eye for an eye and a tooth for a tooth.' But I say to you, do not resist one who is evil.

I am aware of no words of our Lord's that I more wish he had not spoken. These words confound me and offend my moral sense. It seems, and has always seemed to me, that we should recognize and resist one who is evil. And I constantly struggle to understand our Lord's intention. In fact, I want to ignore him or more accurately, find a convincing way to interpret his words so as to be able to ignore him. But I cannot.

If I am truly his adopted brother and he is my Lord and God, then I can only accept this confounding command. The only explanation I can find is that this is exactly how he himself behaved in the presence of his mortal enemies. He declined to defend himself and was silent before the High Priest, Pilate and the crowd that jeered at him and the soldiers who mocked and struck him at his crucifixion. In his passion and death he did not resist the evil men who struck him but turned the other cheek. He prayed for his enemies and those who persecuted him.

When our Lord says, **Do not resist one who is evil**, he is not teaching some obscure moral principle, nor a principle that can be codified in law, nor proclaiming the basis of a new social order. He is asking us to imitate him in his passion and death and in doing so behave as adopted sons and daughters of the God he calls Father.

Reason, moral reason, tells me to resist one who is evil with all my might. My Lord tells me not to. In my heart there is a division, a warfare. Who knows better what's right, me or my Lord? To what end am I to suspend my own judgment and accept his?

The answer is found at the end of today's reading. "You must be perfect as your heavenly Father is perfect." Perfection is not defined by us, but by God, our heavenly Father. It is our Lord, in his words and deeds, who manifests this divine perfection and who is our model.

"You must be perfect as your heavenly Father is perfect," is not a command. It is absolutely impossible for us to fulfill such a command, and I agree completely with Fr. Doran who said last Sunday in his sermon that the Lord does not command us to do the impossible. "You must be perfect as your heavenly Father is perfect" is a promise.

Our destiny as the children of God is to share in our Lord's perfection. Not our imagined perfection but the perfection manifested in our Lord Jesus Christ. And it is in the Sermon on the Mount that our Lord both reveals his perfection and calls us to share in his perfection by imitating him as befits his brothers and sisters adopted in the Spirit. He did not preach the Sermon on the Mount to define a new social order but to reveal his identity and our calling.

43670628R00099

Made in the USA
San Bernardino, CA
22 December 2016